A HISTORY OF THE
VIETNAM WAR

DANTES/DSST* Study Guide

© 2019 Breely Crush Publishing, LLC

*CLEP is a registered trademark of the College Entrance Examination Board which does not endorse this book.

971091818143

Published by Breely Crush Publishing, LLC
10808 River Front Parkway
South Jordan, UT 84095
www.breelycrushpublishing.com

ISBN-10: 1-61433-591-5
ISBN-13: 978-1-61433-591-7

Printed and bound in the United States of America.

*DSST is a registered trademark of The Thomson Corporation and its affiliated companies, and does not endorse this book.

☛ *Table of Contents*

Vietnam Before 1940

ANCIENT VIETNAM: CULTURE, CHINESE INFLUENCE AND INDEPENDENCE

Humans have inhabited the lands of modern-day Vietnam for millennia. In fact, fossilized preserves of *Homo sapiens*' forebears, *Homo erectus*, have been found in caves in Lạng Sơn and Nghệ An provinces that are estimated to be 800,000 years old. Though the transition between *Homo erectus* and *Homo sapiens* is still being investigated, what is clear from the archaeological record is that by around 1000 BCE, these people had begun rice-cultivation, an important progression towards civilization. With it came the specialization of labor and stratification of society indicative of modern man, creating the important Đông Sơn culture that flourished along the Ma and Red Rivers. This culture bound together multiple disparate communities into the Văn Lang and Âu Lạc Kingdoms, the two earliest large-scale political communities in Vietnam.

These two dynasties lasted around 2000 years, roughly from 2879 to 207 BCE, when the Âu Lạc were defeated by Chinese general, Zhao Tuo. Zhao Tuo consolidated these conquered lands into the Nanyue Province, which was composed of modern-day Northern Vietnam and the Chinese Provinces of Yunnan, Guangdong, and Guangxi. This creation of a Chinese vassal state is extremely important to the history of Vietnam, a key event that affected the culture and social structures of the people for centuries to come. Coupled with the already maturing culture of the Vietnamese people, which had been thoroughly strengthened throughout the two kingdoms of Văn Lang and Âu Lạc, and the development of unique political structures, resistance against Chinese rule had begun almost immediately. Though the earliest independence movements, in particular those led by the Trưng Sisters and Lady Triêu, were only successful for short periods, there were other, more successful independence movements. An important movement was led by Vạn Xuân, who successfully defeated the Chinese and ushered in the Anterior Lỳ dynasty that lasted from AD 544 to 602. Yet it wasn't until 938, when the Vietnamese lord Ngô Quyên defeated the Chinese Southern Han state that independence was gained from China after being a vassal state for nearly one thousand years.

The lands formerly under Chinese rule were then renamed Đại Việt—Vietnamese for "Great Viet"—and lived what many historians of Vietnam consider their golden age under the Lý and Trần dynasties. Within 500 years the country had become so politically, economically and militarily able that they were able to successfully repulse three Mongol invasions, a feat matched nowhere else around the world. More importantly, however, was what occurred in terms of religion during this period: Buddhism, the religion that had begun in India in the 5th century BCE and had spread rapidly across the Asian continent, had arrived and blossomed, both literally and figuratively, in Vietnam.

Buddhism became the dominant religion in Vietnam, having little to no competition with other religions until the arrival of Catholicism in the 18th century.

VIETNAM IN THE AGE OF EXPLORATION AND COLONIALISM

Vietnam, by the opening of the European Age of Exploration, had developed a very mature society and culture, both of which were deeply infused with Buddhism, Chinese influences and a tradition of resistance against invasion. However, by the opening decades of the 16th century, internal competition among the Vietnamese divided the country, often breaking out into open and bloody warfare. Within this atmosphere of internecine strife, French missionaries landed on their shores, beginning first with these religious agents—the most important of which was Jesuit missionary, Alexandre de Rhodes, who became the first to attempt to introduce Christianity into Vietnam—then within a short period, economic agents. Through monetary and military support of key political groups in Vietnam, the French were able to slowly insert themselves into the Vietnamese political sphere.

The most important of these political groups was the Nguyễn dynasty, who came to power with French aid in 1802 and lasted until 1945. However, Nguyễn sovereignty lasted for only an historical blink of an eye. In 1858, unification of Vietnam under the Nguyễn ended with the successful attack by French Admiral Charles Rigault de Genouilly on Da Nang, who attacked under orders to stop the persecution of French missionaries. Though at first a mission focused solely on maintaining French Catholic presence, within four years of the major defeat the French continued to push outward from Da Nang, obtaining more and more territory in the process. Vietnam would fall under French control by 1885 after their victory in the Sino-French War (1884-85) gave them Northern Vietnam. By 1893, France had complete control over the lands that came to be called "Indochina," including Vietnam, Cambodia and Laos.

EARLY NATIONALISM AND COMMUNISM IN VIETNAM

Against the backdrop of colonial rule not just in Vietnam but across the world, the tenets of nationalism spread, causing the rise of nationalist parties around the globe. In Vietnam, the Việt Nam Quốc Dân Đảng (VNQDĐ), also known as the Việt Quốc, became the primary nationalist party, adopting a platform that espoused an independent Vietnam from French rule and a socialist economic system. As a result of an internal split, the party had become weakened by late 1929; rather than folding or splitting into multiple groups, VNQDĐ leadership instead planned a rebellion that would sweep the French out in one overwhelming show of force rather than continue its strategy of small-scale guerrilla warfare and high-profile political assassinations, a strategy that brought them widespread attention. On February 10, 1930, the VNQDĐ launched their plan for revolution at Yên Bái, an event that became known as the Yên Bái mutiny.

French forces quickly put down the rebellion, capturing and executing the VNQDĐ leadership.

At the same time these events were occurring, nationalist revolutions and the birth of the Chinese Communist Party (CCP) were forming in China. By the time of the split within the VNQDĐ, however, another party had begun to grow more powerful than the nationalists, who had begun to flee from the party after the mutiny. This party, formed in October 1930 with the unification of the Communist Party of Indochina and the Communist Party of Annam, became known as the Indochinese Communist Party. These two parties, in turn, originated from the formation of the Vietnamese Revolutionary Youth League, established in 1925 by a French-educated Vietnamese student who was born with the name Nguyễn Sinh Cung, who later became known as Nguyễn Tất Thành by the time of the group's founding. With time, Thanh would become Ho Chi Minh, leader of the Vietnamese Communists and the Vietcong after World War II.

Vietnam in World War II, the French-Indochina War and the Cold War

HO CHI MINH: WORLD WAR I-WORLD WAR II, COMMUNISM AND NATIONALISM

Ho Chi Minh was born in central Vietnam on May 19, 1890. In 1911, at age 21, he was able to find work on a French ship as a cook, spending much of the next few years at sea traveling the world. After sailing to Africa, seeing the US and landing in the UK, he settled in Paris, where he would become publicly known within a short period of time. There, he organized a group of Vietnamese immigrants in 1919 and sent a letter to the delegates at the Versailles Conference, petitioning the leaders meeting to negotiate the end of the First World War to force the French Government to grant civil rights to the Vietnamese. The letter was aimed in particular at Woodrow Wilson and the United States, who were directing the negotiations around the focal point of Wilson's Fourteen Points platform. These Fourteen Points, particularly Point V, promoted the principle of popular sovereignty, stating, "A free, open-minded, and absolutely impartial adjustment of all colonial claims, based upon a strict observance of the principle that in determining all such questions of sovereignty the interests of the populations concerned must have equal weight with the equitable government whose title is to be determined." Ho was never able to gain an audience at the Conference, and his letter, which contained a nine-point program for the granting of equal rights to the Vietnamese, was never heard.

The following year, Ho joined the French Communist Party, entering after being inspired by the success of the Bolshevik Revolution and the writings of Vladimir Lenin. He became so well known in the organization, taking part in its activities and becoming educated in Marxist thought, that he was chosen by the French Communist Party to travel to Moscow in 1923. There he was further educated by the Communist International, better known as the Comintern, that was established by Lenin and his associates to spread communism across the world. It is worthwhile to note that central to Marxist-Leninist thought was the belief that communism, once established in one country, would inspire the workers of the world to rise up and take over the means of production; once these were taken, the bourgeoisie—who previously owned the means of production—were overthrown, the workers would rule the world and communism would triumph. However, within a few years of the Bolshevik Revolution, few other revolutions took place, and those few that did failed. In order to spread the Communist Revolution around the world, the Comintern was established in order to train the communists of the world to successfully undertake the revolution in their country.

Before getting into Ho Chi Minh's story following his visit to Moscow in 1923, it is important to address a question that has been debated within the historical community concerning Ho Chi Minh and the Vietnam War: Was Ho a Communist first, using nationalism as a tool to bring communism to Vietnam? Or was the opposite true, that Ho was a Nationalist first, believing that the Vietnamese needed to rule themselves, freeing themselves from the colonial yoke that bound them, before communism could be implemented? Historians generally agree that Ho was a Nationalist first followed by a Communist, but his actual ideology is a little more complicated.

Articles that explored Ho Chi Minh's life at the time of the Vietnam War described Ho as a Nationalist, who believed in a nationalist ethos that called for the people of a nation to rule themselves. Before communism could be implemented in Vietnam, Ho believed, the Vietnamese had to rule Vietnam. In his "Twelve Recommendations," written after the end of the Second World War, Ho stated that "the nation has its roots in the people" and pushed his followers to tap into and spread nationalist principles to the Vietnamese people, who would form the broad basis of support in the decolonialization movement. Only after kicking the French out would communism come to Vietnam.

After his training in Moscow, Ho worked for the Comintern, traveling around Europe to aid in educating and training communist cells across the continent. Along the way, he recruited numerous Vietnamese ex-pats who were being educated in Europe—many of whom went to France to be educated and trained to fill bureaucratic posts in the French Colonial Government ruling Indochina—to a new Vietnamese Communist/Nationalist group. This group became the precursor to the Indochinese Communist Party, founded in 1930 in Hong Kong. He continued these activities throughout the 1930s.

At the start of World War II, Ho Chi Minh became inspired by the German defeat of France and returned to Vietnam in 1941, hoping that an opportunity for Vietnamese independence would present itself with the weakening of the French Government. Shortly after France's defeat, Nazi Germany instituted the Vichy puppet government, which would reestablish itself in Vietnam as the ruling government. Germany and the Vichy Government soon turned over control of Indochina to the Japanese, who used Indochina as a strategic location in taking control of the South Pacific.

This is where Ho Chi Minh and, more importantly, the Chinese come into play in Indochina. Upon his return in 1941, Ho and his lieutenants, Vo Nguyen Giap and Pham Van Dong, organized the Viet Minh, translated into English as the "League for the Independence of Vietnam." Japan's ascension to rule in Indochina created a situation where the ruling government, for a year severely weakened by both the French defeat and the general weakness of the Vichy Government, was replaced by a strong foreign power who was more able to control the people in Indochina. Due to this, Ho Chi Minh and associates turned to the Chinese to get help, thinking that, since the Chinese Government of Chiang Kai-Shek was also at war against the Japanese, they would aid the Viet Minh.

What Ho Chi Minh and the Viet Minh didn't account for was the virulent anti-communist stance of Chiang Kai-Shek and his Nationalist (Kuomintang) Government. By World War II, the Kuomintang had been fighting a communist insurgency that began in the south but moved north after a series of major defeats. Led by Mao Zedong, the Communists and the Kuomintang had developed a United Front starting in 1935, but relations continued to be strained between the two as the communists continued to take and occupy territory after defeating Japanese units. Chiang tossed Ho in jail while, at the same time, lending support to a Chinese-led nationalist resistance movement, the Dong Minh Hoi (DMH), who were tasked with fighting the Japanese across the southern border into Vietnam. While Ho was imprisoned, many of the communists that associated themselves with him and the Viet Minh became active members of the DMH.

The DMH is an important organization for several reasons. The first is the fact that the Chinese hoped to use the group as both a resistance movement in Vietnam against Japan while also gathering intelligence to learn of Japanese intentions in the region. Ultimately, the intelligence gathering failed, prompting the Chinese to release Ho after 18 months in prison. On top of this, the DMH and Southern China became one of the first locations of intense American support and involvement in Asia prefiguring their growing involvement in the region that would come after World War II. In fact, actions undertaken by the Office of Strategic Services (OSS)—the wartime precursor to the Central Intelligence Agency—allowed for the establishment of an intelligence foothold in the region that would be developed later.

FRENCH-INDOCHINA WAR

In August 1945, the Japanese were defeated by Allied forces, leaving Indochina under the control of a provisional government led by Emperor Bao Dai, who would be supported by the French as a puppet ruler upon their return the following year. At the same time, Vo Nguyen Giap, Ho Chi Minh's lieutenant and primary military advisor, led Viet Minh forces into Northern Vietnam and seized Hanoi. They then declared the Democratic State of Vietnam, with Ho Chi Minh as its president and Hanoi as its capital. Emperor Bao Dai abdicated in favor of the revolution, but French troops were able to regain control of the South and maintain Saigon as its capital. It was during this standoff that Chiang Kai-Shek and the Chinese invaded from the north, forcing Ho Chi Minh and the Viet Minh to enter into negotiations with the French.

During the negotiations, Ho implored the French to agree to a Chinese withdraw as well as eventual French recognition of Vietnam's independence. He hoped for a future reunification of North and South Vietnam after French recognition, but events undertaken by the French forced him to abandon the negotiations. In October of 1946, a French cruiser sailing in the waters off of North Vietnam opened fire on the shore, setting off a clash between French and Vietnamese soldiers. Ho attempted to calm tensions and maintain peace, but his more hawkish followers urged war, which broke out officially that December.

French and Viet Minh military strategies differed significantly during the war. The French, who were militarily superior, particularly in armaments, aimed to draw Vietnamese forces out of the villages and jungles towards positions of strength, namely French forts. In order to do so, they hoped for US assistance in providing air power and bombs to use to draw the Vietnamese out and towards the bases. These bases, in turn, would act as Forward-Operating Bases (FOBs) from which to launch offensives into the jungles to root out Viet Minh operatives. They would then establish outposts from which to slowly take control of key areas.

The Vietnamese, led by Giap, were able to develop an effective counter-strategy to French military superiority. It is important to note before we jump into Vietnamese strategy that by the time hostilities broke out, the civil war between the Kuomintang and Chinese Communists had begun to swing in Mao's favor. Within three years, Mao would emerge victorious, establishing the People's Republic of China in 1949. Yet during this time, Mao was able to funnel weapons and supplies from the Soviets south into Vietnam to support the Viet Minh's fight against France.

Giap took advantage of these supplies and weapons to efficiently combat the French through tactics that essentially blocked supplies from reaching French troops. Moreover, Giap and Ho Chi Minh adopted Maoist insurgency principles to recruit an increasingly growing army amongst the people that was further supported by wide political support.

From this, a guerrilla style war was able to be waged against the French, with fighters performing multiple hit-and-run attacks, then sinking back into the jungle and the villages where they were supported by the people. This strategy was continued throughout the 1950s and 1960s, becoming successful not just against the French but the United States as well.

During the Indochina War, however, these tactics culminated in the major victory over the French at Dien Bien Phu. This confrontation occurred among the hills of western Vietnam, close to the border with Laos, where the French attempted to draw out the Vietnamese into the valleys in that region. However, the French made a supreme mistake in choosing the location of the battle, thinking that the Viet Minh would enter the valley and meet them head-on. Instead, prior to entering into contact with the enemy, Giap and the Viet Minh dragged large amounts of heavy artillery equipment into the mountains surrounding the valley, a physical feat almost unmatched in the history of warfare. To top this off, they dug tunnels throughout the mountains and constructed placements for their artillery that would allow greater defense against air assaults from the French. Ultimately, the French had a complete intelligence failure in realizing what the Viet Minh were doing, both an indictment of French military capabilities and an insightful look into the difficulties posed by the geographic landscape.

On the thirteenth of March, the Viet Minh opened fire, laying siege to the French encamped below. At first, the French were able to fly in and drop supplies and reinforcements, but as the Vietnamese became more-and-more successful at shooting these planes down, supplies dwindled. At the same time, fierce ground fighting occurred, with the French largely able to repulse Vietnamese attacks. Slowly, however, the French position contracted, until they were forced to flee the battlefield across the border into Laos. The defeat was resounding and was a key victory not just militarily, but also diplomatically. For, at the same time as the victory, negotiations had already been ongoing in Geneva, providing the Vietnamese the upper-hand in gaining favorable terms from the treaty.

THE GENEVA CONFERENCE AND AMERICAN RESPONSE: SUPPORT FOR CONTAINMENT

The Geneva Conference began as the Battle at Dien Bien Phu was underway. Initially meeting to settle outstanding issues that resulted from the Korean War, the topic of gaining a peace for Indochina was quickly put on the table. Yet the delegates didn't begin until the news of the French defeat at Dien Bien Phu had already arrived in Europe, forcing the French into a weakened negotiating position. By July, the Geneva Agreements had been signed, pushed forward by the crushing defeat of the French, whose days as an empire were largely over.

In the treaty, the French agreed to withdraw troops from Northern Vietnam. The country was to be divided at the 17th parallel for two years until elections could be held, opening the opportunity for the unification of the country under Ho Chi Minh. For this reason, the Americans didn't sign the agreement, but were willing to abide by the treaty conventions. Already knowing the popularity of Ho Chi Minh, the United States was convinced that the country would vote for Ho and the Viet Minh, resulting in the spread of communism into Indochina. This American stance was one that was a perfect elucidation of US foreign policy during the Cold War, a policy of containment.

The strategy of containment began in the immediate aftermath of World War II with the publication of the so-called "X-Article" in *Foreign Affairs*. Written by George Kennan, a Foreign Service Officer working for the US State Department and an expert on the Soviet Union, the article asserted that the "main element of any United States policy toward the Soviet Union must be that of a long-term, patient but firm and vigilant containment of Russian expansive tendencies." The United States had to strive, in Kennan's opinion, to ensure that communism stayed in Russia and Eastern Europe and not spread across the world. This strategy would be the lodestar of American foreign policy beginning with Truman and elaborated on, in different means, by the presidential administrations that followed.

In an attempt to ensure that communism didn't spread to South Vietnam, the United States rushed to develop a policy to strengthen the government of the South. They were able to establish an anti-communist government in South Vietnam under Ngo Dinh Diem while beginning to provide financial and military assistance to bolster the South Vietnamese administration. American involvement in Indochina had begun with money and supplies, a trend that would begin with the Eisenhower administration and ramped-up by President John F. Kennedy. By the time Lyndon Baines Johnson entered office, the United States was so involved that slipping into conflict was almost inevitable.

The United States and Ngo Dinh Diem

The year 1955 was an epochal year in the Cold War. West Germany became its own country; the Soviet Union and seven East European countries signed the Warsaw Pact, the Cold War military rival to NATO; and, most important here, the United States started to send economic aid in the form of $216 million to South Vietnam. At the same time, the Geneva Conference wrapped up, lending a growing urgency by the Americans to act in South Vietnam. To add to this, the theoretical construct of containment began to be further developed, pushing the United States to aid South Vietnam in the struggle against the spread of communism.

US SUPPORT OF NGO DINH DIEM, CONTAINMENT AND THE DOMINO THEORY

To do so, however, the United States had to contend with the problematic, and extremely unpopular, president of South Vietnam, Ngo Dinh Diem. Born on January 3, 1901, in Hue, Vietnam, he was born into a family of aristocrats, his father a minister and advisor to the Vietnam emperor. The family was Catholic and, as a result of their educated status, nationalist. Diem himself was educated at the School of Law and Administration in Hanoi, graduating in 1921, where, as a result of his family status and education, he was appointed governor of Phan-Thiet Province. In this position, he became popular among the people through his land reform program and other policy actions that aided the poor.

He remained as governor until 1933, when he was appointed by Emperor Bao Dai to the post of interior minister for the Commission for Administrative Reforms. He resigned relatively quickly, however, as he recognized the relative powerlessness of the position. It should be noted here that, for Diem, the powerlessness of the position did not mean that he was at a disadvantage or marginalized; rather, the position did not give him the ability to perform any of the reforms he thought necessary and rightful by the title of the position. This reason for his resignation caused his popularity to grow as he was a nationalist in a position of power. He then went into political seclusion for ten years.

Diem would stay quiet for the next ten years until the Japanese arrived. When the country was turned over to the Japanese in World War II, Japan approached Diem to be premier. Again he refused and again he was relatively quiet until the end of World War II. As was told above, events happened relatively quickly in Vietnam following the war. Amid the chaos, with Ho Chi Minh and the Viet Minh taking control of the North and the French attempting to reassert control that Diem shows back up in the historical record. Attempting to return to Hue to convince Emperor Bao Dai to not join forces with Ho Chi Minh, he was captured by the Viet Minh, who imprisoned him. After six months, he was taken to meet Ho, who offered him a position in his government, which Diem refused on account of Ho Chi Minh's communism. Diem soon escaped and traveled to the United States.

In 1953, Diem moved from the United States to Belgium where, at the behest of Bao Dai, he traveled back to Vietnam. He arrived at a point in the history of Vietnam as momentous as the one that he left eight years previously. There, in 1954, Bao Dai appointed him prime minister, a post he accepted quickly. However, within the year, Bao Dai began moving forward with plans to remove him from his post but Diem moved faster. Announcing a referendum to determine the political direction of South Vietnam to be held on October 23, 1955, the referendum gave voters the choice between Bao Dai or Ngo Dinh Diem. Diem won.

Three days later, on October 26, Diem proclaimed the creation of the Republic of Vietnam, placing himself as president. Diem's rule was a textbook example of despotism, but before we jump into the specifics of his rule it is best to lay out general characteristics of Diem that, though already evident, would manifest themselves in his rule. Since his days as a young politician in Phan-Thiet province and in Bao Dai's administration, Diem was a Catholic, a nationalist and a fervent anti-communist. All three of these characteristics would make him both the best ally for the United States at that time and resented by a growing number of people in South Vietnam.

At the same time, and continuing throughout Diem's administration, the United States sent economic aid to South Vietnam, latter upping it to military aid by the opening years of the 1960s. This support, even as Diem became more and more dictatorial wouldn't falter for a variety of reasons, though mostly due to the need to stop the spread of communism to Southeast Asia. The most important advance in containment theory was articulated by Eisenhower's Secretary of State John Foster Dulles and implemented, through Diem, by the United States. This advance became known as the "Domino Theory" which lent the urgency to American actions in Vietnam after the Geneva Convention.

The domino theory is relatively straightforward when it is elaborated in relation to containment. To begin, it must be remembered that communism, particularly Stalin's brand was, by its very nature, dependent upon spreading across the world. By Lenin's plan, the Bolshevik Revolution was supposed to—besides overthrowing the capitalist Provisional Government of Russia—be inspirational to the world's workers to rise up as well. Yet the expected World-wide Revolution didn't come on its own. In order to get it to spread, the Soviet Union developed the Communist International—the Comintern, the agency that trained Ho Chi Minh. To prevent his mission, the United States deployed utilities developed under containment and domino theory. The goal, then, was not just to stop the spread of communism: it needed to be stopped, for if it spread, the country next to it would fall to the ideology, like the next domino in the series.

DIEM'S INADEQUACIES

Diem's presidency was run with the gusto of a small boss surrounded by giant bodyguards, which, all analogies aside, was exactly how he ran South Vietnam. The timing of his ascendancy to the presidency occurred during the two year period before another election was to occur, the nationwide election agreed to by the member-nations of the Geneva Convention. Prior to Diem's "election," the United States had already been undertaking actions to boost up South Vietnam, to support whatever regime could serve as an opposition unit to the North Vietnamese. By 1956, regardless of who the leader was, whatever their personal inadequacies or quirks, the United States was entering a territory they would have difficulty escaping, a veritable no-man's land in international relations.

What the United States got in Diem was a budding tyrant. His first move in office was to refuse to participate in the mandated national elections. Thinking that he would never win in an election against Ho Chi Minh—who was just as popular to many in south of the 14th parallel—he, with the backing of the United States, refused to allow it. At the same time, Ho Chi Minh was willing and ready to go through with the elections, going so far as to ensure that no political activity in South Vietnam would be officially sanctioned prior to the date set for the national election. While the North followed the rules, it was the United States and the Diem Administration that ensured the election wouldn't occur.

To do so, Diem then moved quickly to secure his rule, beginning a period of political repression against any who opposed his regime. As a Catholic, a nationalist and a staunch anti-communist, this was a sizable portion of the nation. The political arrests, executions and terrors mounted against any political opponent or suspected opponent. The numbers of political executions has been estimated at 12,000, with numbers arrested estimated between 35,000 and 40,000. These numbers would continue to rise throughout Diem's rule, from the mid-1950s to early-1960s.

SOUTHERN INSURGENCY AND US COUNTER-INSURGENCY RESPONSE

This opposition was steadily added to by a growing insurgency in the South. Though it had begun in 1954, the insurgency remained sporadic and largely low-scale throughout the countryside. In a strange twist of the tale, this insurgency didn't count for much besides dispersed opposition groups performing small-scale actions against remote government outposts until Diem announced that it was an insurgency. In early 1959, Diem began to act against it, creating Law 10/59 that made it a capital crime to commit a wide-range of political opposition activities. As the law was implemented, opposition groups continued to take political action, undertaking wildcat strikes against the government. Yet it wasn't until January 1959 that opposition groups loyal to the Viet Minh and Ho Chi Minh began to ask for assistance from the North through coordination. North Vietnam finally relented and, in a secret communique, authorized these agents in the South to take military action with Northern aid and supplies. The groups unified and on December 20, 1960 they officially organized the Viet Cong (VC).

The Viet Cong instantly ratcheted up military action, taking control of broad swaths of the countryside. To combat VC activities, the United States and Diem's government developed a tactic that came to be called the "Strategic Hamlet Program," which was fully implemented and financed by 1962. Through the creation of what were called "protected hamlets," the strategy was aimed at isolating the rural population from any contact with the Viet Cong, hoping to cut out the source of political nourishment fueling the rise of the VC. Within these protected villages, the peasants would be given protection and aid by the government which would, it was hoped, build loyalty to the South Vietnamese Government.

To put it simply, the Strategic Hamlet Program, supported with millions of American dollars and growing military aid from the Kennedy Administration, was a failure. Regardless of its inability to combat opposition forces in the rural areas of the South, the Kennedy Administration remained committed to maintaining support of the Diem regime and any actions that was seen as threatening to his regime. After winning the 1960 election, John F. Kennedy's Administration experienced what appeared to be international crisis after international crisis, from the failure of the Bay of Pigs Invasion, to the Cuban Missile Crisis, and to the building of the Berlin Wall. Yet their commitment to containment and their belief in the domino theory established a mindset in the Kennedy Administration that another failure to stop communism's spread would be fatal to American credibility and interests around the globe.

As such, Kennedy and his closest advisors—most notably National Security Advisor Walt Rostow, Defense Secretary Robert McNamara, Director of Central Intelligence Allen Dulles and his brother Robert Kennedy—remained committed to the belief that with enough support Diem could deal with the insurgency. However, in May 1961, Kennedy sent Vice President Lyndon Baines Johnson to South Vietnam, where he pledged not only continued support, but assurances to ramp-up incoming American aid for Diem to build a force to effectively fight the communists. Though not forcing his hand, Kennedy regardless announced a shift in policy, one from ongoing support to partnership with the Diem Administration.

Kennedy's belief that another failure to stem the spread of communism to another state would be, in essence, an existential threat to the United States internally fought against his stance of sending American troops to Southeast Asia. By 1961, however, the Viet Cong were taking control of broad swaths of South Vietnam's countryside, building intense political support due both to the overall inadequacies of the Diem regime and the ability of the Viet Cong and the North to garner support among the peasantry. Though military support through the dispatch of military and intelligence advisors to South Vietnam was not new, Kennedy ramped up this trend, committed to counter-insurgency tactics promoted by both the Pentagon and the Diem Administration. By 1963, the final year of Kennedy's presidency before he was assassinated, 16,000 military and intelligence advisors were being utilized to aid the Diem regime. Kennedy remained committed to counter-insurgency but had been stiffly against any large-scale deployment of American troops.

DIEM COUP

In the meantime, Diem continued to practice repressive politics throughout the South, aiming the repression at any group he deemed an opposition to his rule. Most notably, this included Buddhists, of which a majority of South Vietnamese were adherents of.

After a period of arrests and repression, the political tensions between the Diem regime and Buddhists erupted into the "Buddhist crisis," a period of intense repression on the part of the South Vietnamese Government coupled with a widespread civil resistance campaign led by Buddhist monks. Running roughly from the mid-months to November 1963, the protests originated in the antagonistic policies of the pro-Catholic Diem, who established his government with an inherent bias towards Catholics, allowing them benefits not afforded to the majority of South Vietnamese.

The crisis started over the prohibitory law of flags, a byproduct of a 1958 law that did not allow the use of flags others than the South Vietnamese flag. Vietnamese Buddhist tradition called for the flying of the Buddhist flag on the birthday of the Buddha, and in the political tensions existent in the country at the time, the Diem administration invoked the 1958 prohibition—a law that had almost never been enforced. On May 30, Buddhist monks demonstrated in Saigon, the first major demonstration to have occurred during Diem's rule. After this opening protest, political antagonisms continued to be exchanged throughout the country, leading to widespread attention from international audiences of the repressive nature of the Diem regime.

To add to the troubles of the Diem regime, the South Vietnamese army, even with the overt support of the United States, was abysmal in its performance, the Battle of Ap Bac in January 1963 being the notable example of this continued weakness. Yet, the South Vietnamese forces, particularly those comprised of majority Catholic members who felt themselves above any law, were not just incompetent, but downright brutal. Reported incidences of Diem's paramilitary forces burning pagodas and shooting Buddhists proliferated, culminating in the August 21, 1963 raid by South Vietnamese forces on pagodas across the nation, resulting in widespread destruction and the killings of hundreds of people. Throughout all of this, Diem refused to make any concessions to the Buddhist majority, causing history to lurch from the Buddhist crisis to the ultimate coup and assassination of Diem.

In fact, by 1963, American officials had been discussing the need for a regime change in South Vietnam, though internal disagreements between the State Department (who supported a coup) and the Department of Defense (who supported Diem). The agreed-upon plan was to remove Diem's younger brother who was in charge of the South's secret police and paramilitary units and who, ultimately, was seen as the mastermind behind the Buddhist repressions. While the American officials sent instructions to the US Embassy in Saigon to follow such a move, plans for a coup were already well underway by South Vietnamese military officers. The only thing delaying the overthrow from occurring was the wariness of the generals over possible American reactions. By the end of the summer of 1963, the CIA had been in communication with the generals and clearly communicated that the United States would not stand in the way of any coup attempt. On November 2, 1963, Diem and his brother were arrested and executed, and though the United States did not want Diem executed, officials felt that they would have a greater hand in shaping South Vietnamese responses to the actions of the North.

Lyndon Baines Johnson Americanizes the War

POLITICAL INSTABILITY IN SOUTH VIETNAM

The Diem coup was not the end of political instability in the South. In fact, following Diem's overthrow, sheer chaos ensued across the South, a chaos that was an opportunity for Hanoi, who ramped up their support of southern guerrillas. In fact, calling what occurred in the South following the coup a "political crisis" would be too dull to describe the political instability: in a successive motion, military government after military government replaced each other, playing the domino analogy meant to describe large-scale states out into the real time events of a government. What slowly became evident, with the upped-support of communist guerrillas who continued to view each successive military government as an American puppet—an idea that was quickly accepted by large-swaths of the South Vietnamese population—was that the South had long been politically unstable and divided. Diem's strength as a Nationalist and his willingness to use force to repress opposition, was one of the only things holding it together. Throughout all of this, American military and intelligence advisors continued to advise in almost every level of government in South Vietnam, but were ultimately unable to see the larger political picture, pushing each decision made to be additive to the overall crisis.

ASSASSINATION OF PRESIDENT JOHN F. KENNEDY AND JOHNSON'S FIRST TERM

On Friday, November 22, 1963, President John F. Kennedy was assassinated in Dallas, Texas. Vice President Lyndon Baines Johnson took the oath of office on Air Force One within hours next to First Lady Jacqueline Kennedy; the famous photo taken of the oath shows Jacqueline, next to Johnson, still wearing the clothes she had on when she was sitting next to her husband in the motorcade when he was shot. At the same time, conditions continued to deteriorate not just in Vietnam, as new government replaced new government in the South, but in the United States as well, as the Civil Rights Movement, led by Dr. Martin Luther King, Jr. picked up speed, protesting rampant segregation and racism not just across the Southern United States, but throughout most aspects of American society.

Johnson's first activities as president of the United States revolved around taking care of the domestic political situation. In fact, just days after the assassination, Johnson, in a speech given to Congress stated that "No memorial oration or eulogy could more eloquently honor President Kennedy's memory than the earliest possible passage of the Civil Rights Bill for which he fought so long." Johnson utilized the legacy of Kennedy and the nation's shock at his assassination as momentum to implement legislative plans that had begun with Kennedy but were not fully elaborated or executed until Johnson's administration. This included the landmark Civil Rights Act of 1964 and Voting Rights Act of 1965. As 1964 was an election year, Johnson unfurled his "Great Society" domestic legislation plan in a speech at the University of Michigan, a plan that revolved around passing needed legislation to improve civil rights, urban renewal, anti-poverty, crime control and other reforms.

PRESIDENT JOHNSON, THE GULF OF TONKIN, THE 1964 ELECTION AND THE BEGINNING OF THE CONFLICT

Johnson's domestic legislative actions could have provided him with the status of a great reformer in perpetuity. Yet he is remembered most of all for his escalation of the Vietnam War, an escalation that got the United States so deeply into the conflict there that pulling out would ultimately be an admittance to defeat. In 1963, though publicly drawing attention to those needed domestic reforms, Johnson and his administration's minds were never far removed from the situation in Vietnam. For it was in that year that the political crises racking not only Saigon, but the countryside as well reached to the strategic Mekong Delta, the series of provinces at the farthest tip of South Vietnam— the greatest distance from the 14th parallel in the South. Thus, while Johnson wanted to focus efforts on domestic rehabilitation, he was pressed to continue there. In a speech given on November 24, 1963, he pledged continued support, hinting that aid would be strengthened.

Then came the series of events known as the "Tonkin Gulf Incidents" which gave Johnson an excuse to approach Congress and ask permission to begin introducing American military personnel to South Vietnam. The first of the incidents occurred on August 2, 1964 when the USS *Maddox*, a US Navy destroyer, fired upon North Vietnamese gunboats that it claimed had been stalking them on an intelligence-gathering mission in the Gulf of Tonkin. Two days later, in the same location, the USS *Turner Joy*, another Navy destroyer, reported an attacked by North Vietnamese gunboats. Both of these events would be challenged in the later years by a government document leak—which will be covered later—but due to the reports, the United States retaliated with a series of air strikes against North Vietnamese targets. On top of this result, Congress passed the Gulf of Tonkin Resolution on August 7, 1964, which allowed President Johnson to order military actions in Southeast Asia without a formal declaration of war.

Three months after the passage of the Gulf of Tonkin Resolution was the 1964 Presidential elections, which Johnson won in a landslide against Republican challenger Barry Goldwater. A powerful campaign device employed by the Johnson administration was aimed at Goldwater's continued use of war and nuclear weapons in public speeches, including his proposed use of tactical nuclear weapons in Vietnam. In response, Johnson released a famous national campaign commercial that came to be known as the "Daisy" commercial. Beginning with a little girl plucking the petals off a daisy flower, the camera slowly zooms in on her face as more petals are peeled off. By the time the last is removed, an electronic voice countdown is overheard, and as the number gets closer to zero, the camera zooms in on her eye where, in the darkness, a mushroom cloud erupts. Drawing between Goldwater's flippant remarks on nuclear weapons, Johnson elicited the nervousness of a nuclear attack felt by all Americans—an attack sure to happen if Goldwater became president and used nuclear weapons in Vietnam.

It must be noted that by the time the Gulf of Tonkin Resolutions were passed and Johnson won the 1964 elections, the administration had already decided to continue increasing U.S. military and economic support. The Gulf of Tonkin Incident and Resolutions gave the administration further leeway in a buildup of American troops in Vietnam, particularly ground-troop units from the Marines and Army. US airpower was already being exercised in the region, evinced most fully by the retaliatory air strike campaign against North Vietnamese targets ordered after the Gulf of Tonkin Incident. By the following February, 1965, with the Gulf of Tonkin Resolution in hand, Johnson ordered the commencement of a regular and prolonged series of bombing raids against North Vietnamese targets in a campaign designated "Operation Rolling Thunder."

OPERATION ROLLING THUNDER

Occurring between March 1965 and October 1968, Operation Rolling Thunder was a massive bombing campaign aimed at putting increasing military pressure on the North Vietnamese and eliminating the key routes used by the Viet Cong in entering the country and bringing supplies. In particular, Operation Rolling Thunder was aimed at shutting down what became known as the "Ho Chi Minh Trail," which was a series of roads and pathways used by the Viet Cong to receive supplies from the North. Administration officials believed that the use of continued heavy bombing runs over the countryside close to the 14th parallel would stem the flow of supplies while also encouraging people living along the Ho Chi Minh Trail to end their support of the Communists. On top of this, the Johnson Administration hoped to use the possible successes of the bombing runs to build morale among the South Vietnamese, which would in turn help build stability which could be used to more effectively fight the North.

Over time, air targets were moved deeper and deeper into North Vietnam to continue ramping up pressure on the North Vietnamese Government. It became quickly evident, however, that the North Vietnamese were able to mount effective defenses against American bombing raids and airplanes. This shouldn't come as a surprise: not only did the North Vietnamese have weapons capable of constructing an anti-air defense, but they had used it with mastery almost ten years before at Dien Bien Phu. Moreover, the North Vietnamese continued to receive assistance from the People's Republic of China and the Soviet Union, who helped by giving them newer equipment and by training them. Due to this growing mastery of anti-air defense, the North Vietnamese were able to shoot down hundreds of American fighter jets sent to bomb the North, with the end result being that of all American prisoners taken during the war, the highest percentage was from the Air Force. To add to the problems of bombing North Vietnam, Ho Chi Minh and the Vietnamese simply built a large-scale network of bombproof shelters for the citizenry and constructed tunnels that could be used to further ship supplies south. The ability to continue supplying the South, while protecting their citizens and providing defenses against American bombing runs only served to increase political support for the Communists.

JOHNSON RAMPS-UP THE WAR

In the midst of Operation Rolling Thunder, Johnson also began sending the first American ground troops to South Vietnam. Beginning first with the introduction of 3,500 Marines in March 1965, their first missions were to protect air bases. As Viet Cong attacks against air bases increased, so too did responsibilities to enter combat against the VC increase, which in turn pushed American commanders to call for more troops. By the end of the 1965, however, it became increasingly clear that the United States was not only facing off against the Viet Cong, guerrillas that were born and lived in the areas around the air base. At the same time, the North Vietnamese army began to attack air installations, drawing American troops into combat, particularly around those installations close to the border.

Previous to the entrance of US Marines and the commencement of Operation Rolling Thunder, South Vietnamese forces (ARVN) were dealt a heavy blow by communist forces at the Battle of Binh Gia, which was the first time that the communist forces opted to fight a conventional battle against ARVN. The following June, ARVN forces were again defeated in conventional battle at Dong Xoai, which caused an immense and critical hit on the morale of South Vietnamese forces. As a result, the US Commander of Operations in Vietnam, General William Westmoreland, reported to Admiral U.S. Grant Sharp, Jr. that if morale continued to drop in the South Vietnamese Army and desertions continued to be widespread, the South would be overrun. Taken together with the first moments of contact between American Marines and the North Vietnamese Army, Westmoreland called for a larger deployment of American troops, who would then be able to move from a defensive posture to an offensive campaign. The plan was approved by Johnson in July 1965, which marked a turning point in the war. Westmoreland, confident in a victory with the introduction of American forces, predicted the war would be over by 1967. He was very wrong.

🎓 *America Takes Charge*

Westmoreland's strategy to defeat the North Vietnamese has received numerous critiques, many of which came in the aftermath of the Iraqi insurgency in 2003 as military personnel attempted to develop a counterinsurgency plan. Yet many of these critiques remove Westmoreland's strategy and thoughts from the specific context of Vietnam during the height of the Cold War. It is worth it to remember prior to jumping into the strategy utilized for the first four years of the war (1964-1968) that the immediate enemy—the Viet Cong—were being well-supplied and supported by the North Vietnamese Government under Ho Chi Minh. In turn, the North Vietnamese were receiving aid from the Chinese, their much more powerful and dangerous ally to the north. Westmoreland's strategy aimed at defeating the Viet Cong while insuring against the possibility of another Korea, when American momentum was destroyed quickly by the entrance of the Chinese. In the end, Westmoreland was forced to change the strategy from one of achieving total victory over the Viet Cong to one of attrition to make sure the Chinese stayed out and American casualties remained low.

Upon seeing the morale rates of the South Vietnamese Army (ARVN) drop precipitously in 1965, Westmoreland presented a broad-based, three-part plan to execute the war to Johnson. These phases were not steps but would run concurrently. The first phase dealt with the immediate problem of morale: by introducing American and allied forces into Vietnam, they would provide an army until morale was brought back up. The second part called for a turning of the defensive war into an offensive one, in which U.S. forces would be deployed to fight continual offensive operations that would destroy the forces of the VC. The second phase called, in turn, for an ultimate goal of forcing the enemy from populated areas and away from South Vietnamese citizens. Finally, if this elimination of forces from the cities wouldn't stop the Viet Cong, an additional year would be allocated to mount other offensive actions aimed primarily at enemy bases.

The problems with the strategy were two-fold. The first was that the infiltration of the Communists into the South Vietnamese society was so deep that any attempts to fix morale without confronting the specific societal problems the Communists were promising to solve would end in failure. For the immediate military strategy however, the second issue was more major: neither side was able to wear the other down enough. Continued attacks on Viet Cong positions, followed by VC forces popping up in other locations with greater-or-equal strength established a war of attrition. This type of warfare is extremely old and extremely simple: to win the war, you slowly wear your enemy to the point that their will to fight was no longer there. Cutting off material and troops, surrounding them and forcing them to remain in one isolated place, pushing them into a situation where the onus of citizen responsibility fell on them: each of these were hallmarks of attrition fighting. And as VC troops refused to lose strength or territories, Westmoreland and the United States called in more troops, leading to such a cycle of attrition.

The problems with Westmoreland's strategy didn't end there. At the top of this extensive list was linked to a conundrum. American generals and politicians have found themselves in repeatedly throughout American history: justifying the war and deaths to the American public. To do so, Westmoreland created a rather odd system that measured success: body count. A statistical measure that communicated numbers of enemies killed, the body count success method was one that was particularly well-suited for Defense Secretary Robert McNamara, who was enraptured with statistics and numbers, but terrible for telling the truth about how well a war was going. The amount of territory taken, the psychological impact the fighting was having on your enemy, or intelligence reports indicating that the enemy leadership was moving into the direction of desiring concessions: these are measures of success for a war. In a conflict where the enemy's success rate at recruiting has been known to be quite high, killing as many as possible doesn't properly demonstrate how well the war is going.

Finally, as the United States picked up the deployment rate, foreign goods to support the American military began pouring in to a country whose market had not seen the amount of such goods. A sharp incline of money began pouring in which, in the ideal, would cause more money to go to ordinary shopkeepers and peasants—which in turn would help build loyalty—the money was instead hoarded among the already-elite. Vietnam rapidly went from an extremely poor nation to one with millions of American dollars and goods floating around, causing not just a rapid change in Vietnam's society and economy, but also a sharp increase in public corruption. This public corruption would add to the problems the United States had in finding a suitable governmental partner to build and utilize a strong and loyal army alongside the US.

CONTINUING AIR WAR

In the meantime, the US Air Force continued Operation Rolling Thunder and its subsidiary operations. All of these operations aimed to perform "saturation bombing," an aerial tactic more commonly known as "carpet bombing." In this, the United States continually dropped tons of explosives on both population and unpopulated areas of North Vietnam, aiming to destroy the territory around the Ho Chi Minh trail and Hanoi. Troops on the ground were to enter the bombing location prior to the air offensive and clear out civilians, ideally leaving the enemy combatants in these "free-fire zones." Yet no matter how many millions of tons of explosives were dumped on the Viet Cong and their supply routes, the material and aid never stopped. The objective developed by the chief of staff of the United States Air Force of bombing the communists "back into the Stone Age" didn't work and that relationship between the Viet Cong and North Vietnamese was not divided. Instead, the opposite often rang true: the indiscriminate bombings of the countryside often brought more peasants into the North Vietnamese fold.

STABILIZATION OF SOUTH VIETNAM

Moreover, the political situation in South Vietnam began to stabilize after nearly two years of coups. This final one occurred when Marshal Nguyen Cao Ky and General Nguyen Van Thieu came to power as the dual-heads of a military ruling body in 1965. After a largely fraudulent election, Thieu was elected president with Ky as deputy, though this was largely a public face on an administration run by Ky. However, within two years, Thieu was able to beat Ky behind the political scene, ultimately removing him from power and maintaining his hold on the presidency. He would rule South Vietnam until it was overrun by the North Vietnamese forces in 1975.

AMERICA'S ARMY IN VIETNAM

The war in Vietnam, as has been noted previously, was different from previous wars the United States fought in. The largest departure from the previous wars was that, in trying to deal with the unique warfare first developed by Mao and now exercised by the Viet Cong and North Vietnamese, soldiers were more spread out and mobile. Rather than advancing in large-scale units to attack enemy positions, multiple attack points were undertaken by rapid strike teams throughout Vietnam in the wide-range of geographies present in the country. Indeed, the geography of Vietnam was particularly taxing on the American soldier, who had to deal with a setting with numerous places of cover in order to fully clear out the area in their mission to create "free-fire zones." Coupled with the hit-and-run style of guerrilla combatants, the war took a nasty psychological toll on the soldier, leaving many with Post-Traumatic Stress Disorder (PTSD)—a condition designated and fully articulated during the Vietnam War.

In the end, there were no physical "fronts" to speak of. While soldiers who arrived in the first waves could abstractly pinpoint a front as the perimeter of the air force facilities they were guarding, later military personnel who were sent in every direction, into every village and hamlet, and down into jungles where paths hadn't been created, were never able to say definitively where the enemy was and where his allies were. In fact, the war between 1964 and 1968 had been referred to by military veterans oftentimes as "the good war": a period of conventional fighting against organized North Vietnamese units. After 1968, this melted away, the American G.I. now facing guerrilla fighters who attacked and then disappeared back into the jungle or into villages. To top it off, the guerrilla fighter looked like every other peasant in the country, never wearing military uniforms or sporting military regalia. Confusion over who the enemy was led to fear and resentment and, as a by-product, drug-use and alcohol abuse became a severe issue for the U.S. military. Everyone and no one became an enemy.

Moreover, the soldier began to experience ever-greater levels of psychological trauma as an effect of the values being fought for. While soldiers fighting in the beginning of the war—though not immune from the horror that is war—were still roughly attached to their value system and trusted the United States Government, as the war went on this trust faded. As the trust faded, the average soldier was unsure why he was fighting in a country, what the United States' goal was. The dip in support for the war over time affected the morale of the soldier who, instead of striving for victory for an ideal that was supportable by himself and his family, instead fought only to make it to the date that he would return home. An army without clear-cut goals and a value system to fight for is an army that will lose.

In the "good war," the first major engagement occurred between November 14 and 18, 1965 in Ia Drang, a valley situated in the Central Highlands of South Vietnam. Recall that at the beginning of the war, the strategy was to drive out Viet Cong forces from populated areas by evacuating civilians and leaving enemy forces within the areas to be bombed by Air Force units. Before they could get to these locations, however, they had to drive out Viet Cong and North Vietnamese forces from this region. Westmoreland decided to send the 1st Cavalry Division, a new military unit that incorporated helicopters into its strike plan. It was a highly mobile unit, used to move troops in quickly and drive the forces out before they could rebuff any attack.

SEARCH AND DESTROY: THE BATTLE OF IA DRANG VALLEY

However, in October the North Vietnamese were able to find the locations of the 1st Cavalry Division, launching a failed attack on their positions. In response, Westmoreland ordered the 3rd Brigade of the 1st Cavalry Division to depart from the rest of the unit, find the North Vietnamese, and destroy the enemy. Arriving in the Ia Drang area, they were unable to find the enemy, but acting on intelligence, they learned of North Vietnamese units nearby at Chu Pong Mountain. From there, they are directed to that location on a reconnaissance mission, where they met the North Vietnamese. The North Vietnamese attacked first and were repulsed only after two days of intense fighting, the Americans inflicting heavy losses on North Vietnamese forces.

Then, on November 17, the North Vietnamese were able to overrun the 2nd Battalion of the 7th Cavalry, who were sent to reinforce the 1st Cavalry Division. This was and remained the most successful attack against U.S. forces during the war, more successful than the infamous Tet Offensive that would occur later in the war. Yet the United States were still able to bounce back from this attack, and the following morning the North Vietnamese had left the battlefield, leaving over a thousand casualties against the 250 American G.I.s killed. Westmoreland and his staff, along with the Johnson Administration, reported the incident as a "meeting engagement," a euphemism that belied the fact that, for the first time, the United States had met North Vietnamese forces in conventional warfare. Both sides walked away claiming victory.

Ia Drang was the beginning of a turning point in the Vietnam War. Before we continue, a quote from Ho Chi Minh's close advisor, Vo Nguyen Giap, the brilliant strategist who crushed the French at Dien Bien Phu, is in order for the eerie prediction contained within it:

> The enemy will pass slowly from the offensive to the defensive. The blitzkrieg will transform itself into a war of long duration. Thus, the enemy will be caught in a dilemma: He has to drag out the war in order to win it and does not possess, on the other hand, the psychological and political means to fight a long-drawn-out war.

Giap's quote basically summed up how the rest of the war would play out. Unable to fully defeat the enemy in conventional warfare, the United States would be forced into a unique warily offensive position, sending troops out into Viet Cong-held areas where the warfare was no longer conventional, the enemies were not wearing North Vietnamese uniforms, and all lived among innocent civilians.

 Homefront USA

THE GREAT SOCIETY

After his election in 1964, President Lyndon Baines Johnson attempted to both conduct the Vietnam War, aiming to finish it quickly with the minimum number of soldiers needed in order to maintain the political high ground, and to implement a sweeping domestic legislative agenda. The Johnson Administration titled the agenda the "Great Society," a name he first used in a speech in 1964 at Ohio University in Athens, Ohio. The plan for the Great Society was further unfurled in an oft-remembered speech given as the commencement speaker at the University of Michigan later that year.

The Great Society reform plan, while overarching in its goals and promises, was created and utilized to confront specific problems in the United States. The most important of these was the continued race problem, a severe issue that reached down to the very roots of American society. The Civil Rights Movement had gained overwhelming moral momentum by this point, fueled by their continued protests and the growing television coverage demonstrating the depths of hatred and racism in the southern states to the rest of the country. On top of this most pressing of problems, the Great Society aimed to implement a stable economic plan to counter any possible downturns arising as the postwar economic boom began to fade.

By the time the Great Society was made official, Congressional elections caused a political realignment in the House. Ultimately aiding the passage of Great Society legislation, Southern Democrats (Dixiecrats) were able to undertake actions to get rid of any laws left over from Kennedy's New Frontier program and civil rights legislation, thus placing the focus on Johnson's Great Society legislation. Thus, Great Society programs that created and implemented such items as Medicare, infrastructural fixes and education aid. By the end of 1965, 96% of the bills written and presented were voted on and signed by Johnson, making it the most successful legislative program in US history.

Though ultimately a striking success in legislative action, the Johnson administration continued to face numerous problems, including a continuing Civil Rights Movement after the passage of the Civil Rights Act of 1964 and Voting Rights Act of 1965. The advent of television and the role of the press presented more issues, placing doubt on the administration with their reporting of the war and Civil Rights Movement. The Johnson administration continued to stick by their story that the Vietnam War was going well, domestic programs were being implemented to progress the nation and they were ultimately besting the Soviets in the Cold War. The Civil Rights Movement, the Vietnam War, Congressional dissent and a more educated and connected populace began to create serious problems for the Johnson administration, problems that would ultimately force him to decline running for another term.

THE CIVIL RIGHTS MOVEMENT

By 1964 and Johnson's announcement of the Great Society initiatives, the Civil Rights Movement had gained increasing momentum and support across the United States, fueled by numerous massive protests and continued television coverage. At the same time, opposition to the Civil Rights Movement reached a fever-pitch, with overwhelming violence being conducted daily against African Americans across the United States. To further impress upon the Johnson administration the overwhelming need for federal intervention, massive urban riots erupted in black neighborhoods in New York City and Los Angeles, with the latter being the more famous example.

The Civil Rights Movement was part of a longer history of political agitation and actions conducted by African-Americans throughout late-19th and 20th centuries. These waves of political agitation were focused on eliminating segregation and racism against African-Americans, but prior to the emergence of the concentrated movement in the mid-1950s, political agitation was often aimed at specific sectors where segregation was present. In fact, one of the most important protests was undertaken by female African-American domestic workers. Aiming to gain equality in labor conditions, their protests uniquely spanned the public and private spheres of America, a phenomenon with particular importance to today's United States that is so interconnected through the internet. Moreover, many of these earlier protests—and those that came following 1965—occurred against segregation in the North, a segregation and racism in housing and working conditions that many do not want to remember.

The Civil Rights Movement we know today, then, is a culmination of a long history of political agitation against segregation and racism. Emerging in the mid-1950s, the first major protest surrounded Rosa Parks and the subsequent Montgomery Bus Boycott of 1955-1956. In the following years, protests would be taken to de-segregate schools and universities across the South in accordance with the Supreme Court ruling in *Brown v. Board of Education* (1954), desegregation of public buildings and parks, and against restrictive voting laws disenfranchising African Americans. The movement at heart was one of peaceful civil resistance, promoting its cause through continued acts of nonviolent protest and civil disobedience.

Multiple factors became important to the success of the Civil Rights Movement. The first was due to the leadership of Dr. Martin Luther King Jr. and others and the organizational skills developed and implemented by civil rights organizations such as the NAACP, the Southern Christian Leadership Conference (SCLC) and the Student Nonviolent Coordinating Committee (SNCC). The second factor was the ability of these organizations and leaders to conduct protests that forced the response of government authorities across the South; these responses, often done immediately with very little thought to their effects, were conducted with often overarching violence and hatred. Finally, the third factor was one that would affect not only the Civil Rights Movement, but the war in Vietnam as well: television. As televisions became more commonplace in households across the United States, more and more Americans were watching not only the destructive images coming out of the war in Vietnam, but also the levels of violence being conducted against African-American protestors. Support continued to rise for all of these reasons.

Ultimately, the Civil Rights Movement was able to force the United States Government to pass a series of laws, rule on key anti-segregation laws and create multiple agencies for civil rights oversight. The most important of the laws were the Civil Rights Act of 1964 that outlawed discrimination based on race, color, religion, sex or national origin and the Voting Rights Act of 1965 that prohibited racial discrimination in voting. Supreme Court rulings included the overturning of the "separate but equal" doctrine established by *Plessy v. Ferguson* (1896) in *Brown v. Board of Education* (1954), which ultimately ruled the creation of separate black and white public schools and buildings to be unconstitutional, and *Loving v. Virginia* (1967) that legalized interracial marriage. Finally, key federal agencies were created to provide federal oversight and assistance against segregation and racism, including the Civil Rights Division of the Justice Department (1957), the Equal Employment Opportunity Commission (1965) and the Office of Fair Housing and Equal Opportunity in the US Department of Housing and Urban Development (1968).

Though these were landmark successes, segregation and racism continued throughout the United States in the aftermath of the Civil Rights Movement. By the late 1960s, the movement began to have internal divisions between those aiming to continue conducting peaceful political agitation and those promoting violent means—most often defensive violent means. Moreover, the movement began to travel north to protest segregation in housing and working environments: for example, Martin Luther King Jr. was in Memphis to speak to protesting black sanitary public works employees, while simultaneously planning a "Poor People's March" to protest northern segregation, when he was assassinated in 1968. Other organizations and movements began in its immediate wake, including the Black Panthers and Black Power, and movements active today—most notably the BlackLivesMatter movement—find its routes in both the Civil Rights Movement and the movements that followed.

TELEVISION, THE DRAFT AND THE CREDIBILITY GAP

On top of the Civil Rights Movement, three themes converged to cause immense problems for the Johnson administration. The first was the dual role of the press and the advent of the television. Though television began to become popular in the 1950s, its take-off as a staple of every American household did not begin until the 1960s. In fact, televisions growing role as the prime means of media communication had a direct correlation to the increased news programs from Vietnam. By the end of the 1960s, the Vietnam War began to be known as the "Television War," a designation that belied the crucial role television had in changing public perceptions of the war and the politics of the 1960s.

Television crews arrived in Vietnam with the initial wave of troops in 1965. Battle-after-battle, death-upon-death: images rolled down on the American public like the bombs dropped from the US Air Force upon the Vietnam countryside. While the American public had watched combat footage of the Second World War and the Korean War, the footage was often from afar, showing images were shot from high in the sky or in the aftermath of battles. As the conflict in Vietnam stretched on, dead and dying American soldiers were coupled with the sheer chaos and horror that was war. The most vivid occurred almost immediately with the start of the war, the August 1965 CBS special presented by Morley Shafer that showed Marines lighting the roofs of the homes in a Vietnam village. To add to this, Shafer provided interviews and commentary that detailed the violent treatment of the villagers by US troops and their allies. These images were sure to cause revulsion and turn the opinion of the American public against the war.

This public antipathy towards the war would take years to fully develop, but the initial disgust against the conflict occurred first in the highest levels of government. From the start, the United States Government and military aimed to control the media coverage of the war by keeping media crews and military journalist teams locked into stories that showed the United States winning the war. Intrepid journalists, like Morley Shafer, were able to provide news stories showing another, darker side of the war, a side that provided a contradictory picture of the war then the one presented officially by the Johnson administration. Over time, the media coverage and that official stance continued to divide into a widening gap, resulting in what was labeled the "credibility gap." Ultimately, this caused public trust in the Johnson administration to drop and, later, to cause a crisis of faith in the United States Government.

The first disruption in trust occurred between the executive and legislative branches of the federal government, in which Johnson continued to refuse to give a straight answer on how the war was going. Indeed, as the war progressed, Johnson and the Pentagon stuck to their story that the war was being run, but as the months passed more news stories came out communicating that the United States was losing. This was coupled with the fact that popular opposition to the war was growing rapidly and, as a rather striking political statement of opposition, individuals began to "draft-dodge," meaning they refused to be conscripted into the growing military forces being sent across the Pacific. As we will see below, opposition to the Vietnam War, though predating the start of the conflict, the television coverage, and the credibility gap, was rapidly growing, causing further problems for the United States Government and contributing to the growing crisis that characterized the mid- to late-1960s.

OPPOSITION TO THE VIETNAM WAR: INTELLECTUALS, POLITICAL AGITATORS AND HIPPIES

Opposition to the war began on a small-scale with leftist intellectuals in 1962, but did not begin to quicken until demonstrations began in 1964. Starting on college campuses, the first major opposition organization was the Students for a Democratic Society (SDS) who began politically agitating against the war through a series of "teach-ins," protests reminiscent of the sit-ins being conducted by the Civil Rights Movement. The SDS was the most visible and active element of what became known as the "New Left," an intellectual and political movement that encompassed a broad range of radical ideals, like Marxism. On top of the teach-ins, student radicals conducted opposition campaigns on college campuses, with particularly acute and popular protests occurring at the University of California, Berkeley, and the University of Michigan.

At the same time that the New Left and radical organizations began to develop and became popular on college campuses, artists, musicians, and public intellectuals further took up the mantle to oppose the war. Opposition sentiments swept through the music and lyrics of popular musicians like Bob Dylan, Joni Mitchell, Joan Baez and Jimi Hendrix. Poetry from Allen Ginsberg, Robert Bly and David Ray spoke out against the conflict. Yet, one of the most poignant examples of artists using their specific mediums to communicate opposition came from photographers, in particular Ronald Haeberle, whose images of the My Lai Massacre set off wide-spread consternation amongst the American public, further building opposition.

As this political opposition grew so too did a social movement that grew out of the rising usage of recreational drugs, new music and an anti-establishment mentality: the hippies. The hippy movement began before the 1960s, originating in the 1950s with the members of the "Beat Generation," a literary movement that developed a lifestyle around anti-establishment ideals. Rising up with the wave of jazz music that was rapidly moving away from the big band sound of the 1940s, popular commentators began to refer to them as "hipsters," a name that shifted over time into the hippie. This particular counterculture thread created separate communities apart from the rest of American society, consumed drugs such as marijuana, LSD, and psilocybin mushrooms, and played a new style of rock-and-roll they aptly called "psychedelic."

Together these groups comprised what came to be known as the counterculture movement, a designation that has been repeatedly used since the 1960s to describe any cultural group that goes against the major culture. Major countercultural groups were born and rose in major cities around the world, notably San Francisco, London and New York City. Ultimately, the countercultural movement was deployed as an umbrella term that encompassed a wide-range of socially progressive groups from anti-war protestors, to feminists, to hippies. As the movement spread and brought in more groups, it became more accessible to a wider-range of the American public. As they sat and watched the news coming from Vietnam, these Americans would rapidly join the ranks of those who opposed the war.

 # Tet and Its Aftermath

If ever there was a watershed moment in the Vietnam War, it was the Tet Offensive. Named after the Vietnamese New Year's holiday, the Tet Offensive was a surprise attack undertaken by the North Vietnamese across the nation. When the North launched this coordinated attack against US and South Vietnamese military centers and cities, it was the culmination of months of planning. Though the US and South Vietnamese military were able to repulse the attack, the overwhelming force, the surprise and the images of violence and destruction that were delivered by news teams on the ground was the last battle prior to an overwhelming opposition to the war by the American public.

VIETNAMESE PLANNING

The context in which the North planned the Tet Offensive—and their goals in undertaking it—were closely tied to the direction the war was going in. In particular, both belligerents were engaging in a war that was quickly coming to a stalemate, the United States dealing with the problems inherent in the credibility gap written about above and the North recognizing the dangers of a war against a technologically superior foe.

For the North, the destructive force of the American military machine was beginning to overwhelm not just the Viet Cong and North Vietnamese Army, but also the morale of the populace.

Yet the Communists had one paradoxical weapon in their pocket that they had been using rather sparingly, but were to unleash with Tet: the American public. It should be recalled here that Ho Chi Minh and General Giap understood that, if they drew the war out and held out for long enough, they could get the American public to turn against the war. Moreover, the context in which it was being planned was one that was a race between striking a blow at the morale of the United States and an overwhelming loss of morale amongst Vietnamese citizens, a race that they were losing. The Tet Offensive then suggests a major gamble by the North, but it was a smart gamble: they needn't necessarily win the battle, but do just well enough to strike a serious blow against the morale and support of the United States and its allies.

The ultimate goal of the Tet Offensive, then, was to strike a blow at the morale of the United States and to convince more people in South Vietnam to support the Communists. Believing that a surprise attack had the opportunity to force a military collapse, Giap chose the Tet holiday as a day when the South would let their guard down. The offensive, however, started ten days previously to the January 31st Tet holiday: by attacking the Marine base at Khe Sanh, the Vietnamese drew the attention of Westmoreland and the American military away from target areas. The battle for Khe Sanh , if not overshadowed by the Tet Offensive ten days later, would have been one of the most important battles of the war, except that it was nothing more than a diversion.

THE TET OFFENSIVE

Finally, on the morning of January 30, 1968, the attack began. The Viet Cong were ordered to attack major cities largely in the central region of South Vietnam. The attack took the South Vietnamese by surprise as many had just begun their New Year's celebrations. Yet again, however, this was diversionary and meant more to weaken key defensive areas. The following morning, a combined North Vietnamese Army and Viet Cong force attacked a large number of other targets in a series of over one hundred attacks. The attack that took up the most attention of the Americans in the aftermath of the Offensive was the attack by a Viet Cong platoon on the American embassy in Saigon. The attack was only thwarted when the Marines guarding the complex ordered it destroyed after evacuating the personnel.

Ultimately, Giap was able to surprise the Americans and South Vietnamese, but due to how many targets he attacked, he was unable to claim a military victory. Yet he was able, in a way, to claim that partial victory of which they aimed from the outset, causing widespread fear and consternation amongst the American public. Furthermore, though the January 31st attacks would be remembered in American history, the attack against the southern city Hue (the same city from which Diem came from) lasted for over three weeks, claiming the lives of thousands of Viet Cong and North Vietnamese soldiers, close to 400 South Vietnamese troops and civilians, and 150 U.S. Marines.

TET: THE AFTERMATH

As stated before, the Tet Offensive was both a strategic victory and a military defeat for the North. In particular, up to that point in the war, President Johnson and William Westmoreland were able to maintain the story that the war was being won with some semblance of justification, particularly due to the body count statistics. The central message, wrapped up in these justifications, was that the war was being won and it a victory within the following year would be achieved. Tet ruined this vision, proving to the American public that the war would not be quick but spectacularly drawn-out. If political support was money, the Johnson administration didn't just not have enough money to conduct such a war, but were quickly going bankrupt.

Almost immediately, war opposition grew, now entering the Johnson Administration itself. Indeed, by the end of February, Secretary of Defense Robert McNamara stepped down; his replacement, Clark Clifford, had already publicly supported a draw-back of American forces. From that point on, the Johnson administration was fighting a losing battle justifying the war to the American public and his actions following the Offensive was largely one of retreat and defeat. First, on March 31st, he called for a drawback of American bombing runs and announced that he would approach the North to begin peace talks. Then, in a telling move that showed the defeatism running through his administration, he announced that he would not seek reelection in the November 1968 presidential elections.

 The War at Home

THE 1968 ELECTIONS: A TENSE NATION, A COLLAPSING DEMOCRATIC PARTY AND THE RISE OF NIXON

Johnson's announcement that he would not seek reelection came as a surprise, seeing as it came at the end of the March 31st speech pronouncing a drawback to the bombing of Vietnam and an entrance into the peace talks. This was only the first event that threw the 1968 elections into turmoil. Indeed, the 1968 election was one of the most contentious amid one of the tensest years of American history. As opposition to the war mounted, political demonstrations became more frequent and often times more violent. Political violence and riots swept the nation in the wake of the Martin Luther King and Robert Kennedy assassinations. Campuses remained hotbeds of political agitation resulting in the growing radicalization of student bodies the nation-over.

While Johnson was still president, even prior to his announcement, other candidates began to put their names out for consideration, with an initial split in popularity between John F. Kennedy's younger brother and former Attorney General Robert Kennedy and Eugene McCarthy of Minnesota. McCarthy's political star would soon fade as Kennedy became more popular, especially among the poor, minorities and Catholics. However, the entire race changed minutes after midnight in a hotel kitchen in Los Angeles when Kennedy was gunned down after giving a campaign speech. The entire Democratic field opened up to fierce competition, to be played out at the Democratic National Convention that convened in Chicago in August 1968.

Yet the real show occurred outside the Convention. There, a massive protest led by the National Mobilization Committee to End the War in Vietnam, the Youth International Party—commonly called the Yippies—and the Students for a Democratic Society convened in Grant Park to hold a massive rally in front of the Convention. Chicago mayor Richard J. Daley, however, had different plans: aiming to showcase his city to the national politicians arriving to take part in the Convention, he had no room in his plans for these protests. He thus sent the police out to arrest and contain them, intending to keep them away from the Convention. After several arrests, things turned violent, and as the cameras rolled, the protest quickly turned into a riot. Images and events like this ultimately affected not just the Convention but ultimately the elections.

Meanwhile, at the Republican National Convention held in Miami, Florida, Republicans conducted a nomination that was anything but chaotic. After one round of balloting the Republic Party unified behind Richard Nixon, who had also been tapped as the nominee in the 1960 election, where he was defeated by John F. Kennedy. Nixon laid out his strategy immediately, calling for a platform of law and order and a return to the diplomatic style of Eisenhower, whom he had served under as Vice President. This new diplomatic approach aimed to bring new leadership on the Vietnam War, a veiled promise to find a diplomatic solution to the war where Johnson's had failed. Finally Nixon's campaign aimed to get the votes of what he would later call the "silent majority"—a term he used to refer to those who opposed both the war and the countercultural movement's tactics in opposing the conflict. He would ride this campaign to victory.

President Nixon's First Term: A Country Filled with Tension

President Nixon's first term in office was hardly any easier than Johnson's final years. Within that first year, Nixon had to face ongoing political demonstrations, most notably the Moratorium to End the War in Vietnam, and college campuses that were becoming more violent, culminating in the Kent State massacre in May 1970. Nixon's first Thanksgiving in office in 1969 was spent putting out the political fires that resulted from the release of information in the news about a massacre committed by American troops in two Vietnamese hamlets that became known as My Lai. The war meanwhile continued, spreading into Cambodia and Laos as the United States tried to shut down the Ho Chi Minh Trail. Then, like a cherry on the cake, a classified report that came to be known as the "Pentagon Papers," which detailed how the American Government under Johnson had been continually lying about how well the war was going was released.

This is not to say that the Nixon Administration didn't have moments that ultimately benefited the American public. Notable among these were the diplomatic breakthroughs achieved by Nixon and his cabinet, particularly Henry Kissinger, who served first as his National Security Advisor and later as his Secretary of State. Ending the War in Vietnam and thawing relations with China were two notable foreign policy achievements of the Nixon administration. These breakthroughs will be covered later in the chapter as we wrap up the war.

The first major problem that the Nixon administration faced occurred on October 15 and November 15, 1969. Beginning with a nationwide teach-in and march that drew thousands of demonstrators, the Moratorium to End the War in Vietnam resulted from two threads, the first part of a longer trend and the second more immediate. As can be readily seen throughout this chapter, political protests against the war did not slow down, neither after Johnson's call for drawbacks in bombing campaigns and attempt at entering peace negotiations nor after Nixon's election. Then, in April 1969, Jerome Grossman, a major voice in the anti-war movement, called for a massive, nationwide strike if the United States had not ended the conflict by October; it was scaled back to a Moratorium by other activist leaders who had an eye on getting as many people as possible to participate. A month after the initial protest, a second, and much larger, political demonstration was held that brought over 500,000 people to Washington.

At the end of November, another story quickly surpassed news of the Moratorium, though it would in no way take away the political momentum from the anti-war movement. Though the event had happened nearly two years prior, an interview with a former-US military official telling the public about a massacre in a village in Vietnam surface. Almost immediately, pictures taken by photographer Ronald Haeberle were splashed across the front pages of almost every major news agency of the country. Showing the bodies of countless Vietnamese peasants, the public soon came to learn about an event the United States Government tried to cover up: an American platoon had massacred scores of Vietnamese in two hamlets in a village called Son My. The incident quickly began to beknown by the name of one of those hamlets: the My Lai Massacre.

Though a few reporters had independently found out about the incident, the Johnson Administration was at the height of its ability to control the flow of information out of Vietnam, cutting the story off before it could be explored. The Defense Department stepped in as well, beginning efforts to cover up the massacre. But the story still broke and the Johnson administration was forced to order an investigation. The investigation was led by a 31-year-old Army officer who would later serve as Secretary of State: Colin Powell.

What his investigation found out was that the incident began with orders to raid the village of Son My based on reports of Viet Cong guerrillas hiding in the village. Led by Lieutenant William Calley, the unit's morale had become severely weakened due both to the Tet Offensive and because more than twenty men in their unit had been killed by VC attacks and booby traps in the short period they had been deployed. They were told by their coming officers that the village was to be destroyed and any soldiers found to be arrested. They found no soldiers, but hundreds of ordinary villagers. Their anger had turned to sheer fury and hatred, and they rounded up the villagers and began to torture, rape and murder them. The massacre only ended when an Army helicopter pilot landed the chopper between the fleeing civilians and the chasing troops, threatening to open fire if they continued.

Ron Ridenhour, the soldier who related the story to journalists two years later, though never taking part, nonetheless heard about the incident from fellow troops and fought to make the story known. The images only showed so much, but Ridenhour's story to investigative journalist Seymour Hersh, which was reprinted and analyzed across the country, filled the public in on the major parts prior to details of the investigation were released. In the end, the troops were later court-martialed, all of whom were found not guilty—on the defense that they were following orders—but Calley was convicted and sentenced to twenty years. The sentence was later reduced to ten years and he was exonerated in 1974.

Many commentators viewed Calley's conviction and imprisonment as the government and military scapegoating him. Anger over the massacre and its aftermath was further compounded by the government cover up of the massacre, further fracturing any trust the public had in the United States Government. Nixon's job up to this point lay primarily in cleaning up the mess left over by the Johnson Administration and restore trust in the government to build and maintain legitimacy. However, within the next two years, the mess would grow much larger with two major events, one of which was blamed directly on the Nixon administration: the Kent State Massacre and the leak of the Pentagon Papers.

On the morning of May 4th, 1970, students at Kent State University in Kent, Ohio began protesting the commencement of military operations in Cambodia, which had been announced on national television earlier that week by President Nixon. Protests against the continued involvement of the United States had started on the first of May, not just at Kent State, but at campuses across the nation. Shortly after the protestors dispersed, they traveled to the town of Kent and after drinking in the local bars, began to throw beer bottles at passing police cruisers and vandalized local business. Tensions between the students and the citizens of the town were thus very high when the protests began. Police were sent out and the mayor of Kent called in assistance from the National Guard. Composed primarily of young men that were roughly the same age as the protestors, they opened fire on the protesting students, killing four instantly and injuring nine others.

News of the massacre traveled quickly. Aided by reporters and photographers on the scene—including John Filo, who snapped the Pulitzer Prize-winning picture of 14-year-old Mary Ann Vecchio crying out over the body of Jeffrey Miller. Student strikes occurred across hundreds of campuses and the outcry across the country was swift and indignant. To top it off, the Nixon Administration responded at first with almost callous carelessness. After a later shooting of two other students at Jackson State University in Mississippi, Nixon was forced to respond, which he did by establishing the President's Commission on Campus Unrest. The report, released later that year, told the country something it already knew: the shootings were unjustified.

Then in February 1971, a former Defense Department contractor named Daniel Ellsberg approached *New York Times* reporter Neil Sheehan with 43 volumes of a highly-classified report. Written for the Johnson Administration under the orders of then Secretary of Defense Robert McNamara, the report was a detailed study of American involvement in Vietnam from 1945 to 1967. The information contained within the report, compared to the official narrative presented by the federal government, told a pretty straightforward truth: the American Government had been lying to the public about both the depth of American involvement and, most importantly, that the war had been almost un-winnable since the beginning.

After *The New York Times* published three articles, the Nixon Administration stepped in and ordered the newspaper to stop printing. Claiming that the articles posed a risk to national security, Nixon ordered the Department of Justice to issue a restraining order. Debates had occurred as well within the offices of the major newspapers who received the leaked documents—most notably *The New York Times* and *The Washington Post*—but ultimately both newspapers' staff believed that the American public needed to know what the reports contained. This, in their minds, outweighed any threats to national security that were still present and, after the Nixon Administration took them to court, the justices on the Supreme Court largely agreed with the journalists, ruling that the government had not provided enough proof of the stories posing a threat to national security.

As a result of the stories, much of the remaining support the American people had for the war quickly evaporated. Luckily for Nixon and his administration, American foreign policy during this period offered a variety of important breakthroughs that gave him political points with the public. These breakthroughs included the "Vietnamization" of the war, the "opening" of China, a small détente with the Soviet Union, and eventually the ability to withdraw from Vietnam. In the aftermath of this final "success" for the Nixon White House, the North invaded into the South, eventually defeating the South Vietnamese Army and conquering Saigon. The last American personnel, as well as a few Vietnamese who were loyal to the United States, fled the country, much as the American military was forced to.

American Foreign Policy in the Age of Nixon

Within months of his election, Nixon began plans to withdraw from Vietnam. His original goal aimed for a phased exit from the country while simultaneously training and supplying the South Vietnamese Army to fight any threats from the North and Viet Cong—a strategy not unlike the counterinsurgency strategy developed by General David Petraeus in the Middle East close to ten years ago. Named "Vietnamization," the goal was to begin withdrawing a majority of the American military personnel stationed there by the Spring of 1971. In order to further communicate American plans to turn the war over to the South and allow them to fight their own war, Nixon ordered B-52 bombers loaded with tactical nuclear weapons to fly over China and the southern USSR. The message was clear: back off from Vietnam and let them fight their own war.

Yet carrying through with his plans would become increasingly difficult, as actions in the region pushed Nixon to continue military campaigns while moving troops from the border regions to the interior. For it was by this period that the two countries bordering Vietnam—Cambodia and Laos—began to become additional battlegrounds as the war spread, largely due to attempts by the North to extend the Ho Chi Minh Trail. The interconnected histories of these former French colonies forced the expansion of the war at a time when it was supposed to be contracting. Ultimately, the war would have to be expanded before it could be finished, but, at the same time, the relationship between the United States, China, and the Soviet Union began to turn around for the better, pushing this expansion away from the American public before the 1972 elections.

CAMBODIA AND LAOS

After the signing of the Geneva Convention, Cambodia's ruler, Prince Narodom Sihanouk, made repeated public pronouncements of his country's neutrality. However, the North Vietnamese Army and Viet Cong continued to use the rural areas in the border regions between Cambodia and Vietnam as routes for the Ho Chi Minh Trail and locations of camps and bases. Even with his stance of neutrality, Sihanouk ignored their presence until he was pressured by the United States to end his passive attitude towards the VC and kick them out in 1969. Almost immediately upon this change in policy, Nixon moved forward with a bombing campaign against communist positions, both along the border and within Cambodian territory in "Operation Menu."

Prior to the commencement of Operation Menu, Cambodia had been having severe domestic problems, culminating in a near civil war between the US-backed government and the Communist-backed Khmer Rouge. By the time Nixon began Menu, an internal coup had overthrown Sihanouk and Lon Nol, Sihanouk's prime minister and favorite of the Americans, came to power. Soon after, the North ramped up their support of the Khmer Rouge that eventually resulted in the North Vietnamese Army invading Cambodia to defeat Lon Nol's government and install the Khmer Rouge, led by future despot Pol Pot, as leaders of the country. In line with containment and the domino theory, the Nixon administration ordered US and South Vietnamese forces to deploy across the Vietnam/Cambodia border to push back the combined North/Khmer forces. As in Vietnam, they were unable to do so, which eventually resulted in a Khmer Rouge victory, an installment of Pol Pot as leader and an eventual genocide in Cambodia between 1975 and 1978.

Along with the invasion of Cambodia, the North moved the war into Laos, aiming at extending the Ho Chi Minh Trail into a country that would, in turn, open another front closer to key South Vietnamese positions. Yet again the Vietnamese were entering a territory that was being torn apart by a civil war. And yet again, the United States and North were using another country's domestic strife as a proxy war against each other, much as they did prior to full out invasion in Cambodia. In the end, to put it simply, Laos was a disaster for the invading South Vietnamese Army and a massive cleanup and loss of supplies for the Americans. In fact, at the first sign of resistance, South Vietnamese forces turned and fled back toward the border, eventually running out of fuel and leaving behind American equipment. The US was then forced to destroy the equipment before it fell into enemy hands. It was at this point that American troops, now severely demoralized, were withdrawn back into their positions, facing the last offensive moves of the war.

Later that year, between July and October 1971, Nixon's national security advisor, Henry Kissinger, made several trips to China on diplomatic missions. Prior to his trips to the People's Republic, the Nixon administration had succeeded in opening up better communication and slightly better relations with the Soviet Union, a process referred to in political science as "détente." However, the détente did not achieve all of the goals the United States had in mind when they entered into discussions. The Cold War, it seemed, would remain cold.

However, Kissinger's visits to plan a future diplomatic visit by Nixon to China provided possibilities for future negotiations with the Soviets. Approaching and opening up diplomatic channels and better relations with the Chinese offered numerous advantages for the United States. At the top of this list was the addition of some other international actor with clout in Asia that could be negotiated with to achieve strategic aims; no longer would they only be able to work through the Soviets, but could negotiate with the Chinese for better deals. Next to this was the ability to use the Chinese as a strengthening catalyst in future negotiations with the Soviets. This plan was to use the opening of good relations with the Chinese to exploit the Soviet Union's paranoia of actions occurring, in their regional neighborhood, that would risk their interests. Finally, and most pressing of all, the Chinese and Mao Zedong were more important to the North Vietnamese, which would allow the Chinese to help bring Ho Chi Minh to the negotiating table to end the war.

Kissinger's trip was to set up a meeting between Nixon and Mao, a meeting that the Chinese readily accepted. The following February (21-28) 1972, President Nixon stepped off an airplane to meet with Chinese leaders. Almost immediately upon landing, Nixon was called to meet immediately with Chairman Mao and his top lieutenant, Zhou Enlai, to discuss a wide array of diplomatic and political issues. Unbeknown to Nixon and those sitting in on the meeting, Mao was in poor and declining health (he would die four years later, in 1976, as a result of the lung and heart ailments that were caused by his heavy smoking), but by the end of the meeting, he and Zhou Enlai were able to effectively communicate China's stances on a number of issues. These stances were easily worked with, and by the end of the trip, they were able to successfully agree to the biggest issue that had been serving as an impediment to any future diplomatic relationship: a peaceful settlement on Taiwan. This ultimately brought the Chinese in as a third-party to urge the North to enter peace negotiations.

"A Decent Interval": Nixon's Second Term

Nixon's trip to China was a smashing political and PR success. Ensuring that all of the major moments would have television coverage, Nixon essentially swung the political pendulum back in his favor. Though good relations with China would pick up speed in 1974 following Nixon's resignation, the sheer fact that he was willing to approach China to create better relations played well with American voters. Then, a month before the November 1972 election, the Nixon administration announced that they had reached a cease-fire agreement with the North. The war appeared to be coming to an end, and Nixon rode this to a sweeping victory to be reelected.

Yet within days of the announcement, South Vietnamese leader General Thieu began to demand changes in the cease-fire agreement that would have defeated the purpose. The North, then, went public with the exact wording of the agreement. To bring both sides to the table, Nixon ordered a bombing run to further damage the North's economy, giving confidence to Thieu in favorable future negotiating terms and demonstrating to Ho what continued resistance would leave him. Finally, on January 15, 1973, Nixon announced the end to hostilities. The cease-fire was put into effect on January 27 after the signing of a treaty, and the United States was given 60 days to withdraw from the country.

The treaty, officially titled "The Agreement on Ending the War and Restoring the Peace in Vietnam," but more commonly referred to as the "Paris Peace Accords," ended direct American involvement in Vietnam. Essentially leaving the South to defend itself, the agreement called for a 60-day withdrawal window, a temporary cease-fire and an exchange of prisoners. Yet even before the cease-fire period was up, the South, now very well supplied by a parting gift from the American military, began to use force to successfully push the Viet Cong out of their positions back towards the North. However, after the South gained several victories over Viet Cong and North Vietnamese forces, the North organized the "Great Spring Offensive" in 1975, an offensive unmatched in the rest of the war. They were able to push back the South Vietnamese back to Saigon, where the South put up a rather determined defense. In the end, though, it wasn't enough and on April 30, 1975, Saigon fell.

Prior to the beginning of the Great Spring Offensive, but after the withdraw of American forces from Vietnam, the Nixon Administration began to fall apart. To begin, the administration's power, indeed the power of the executive branch, was sharply curtailed by the passage of the War Powers Act, a federal law that aimed to remove the president's power to place American troops into combat without getting approval from

Congress. Presidents have broken this law numerous times, particularly as modern warfare calls for the use of special operations forces whose specialty is in quick missions that can be completed covertly.

Then, in 1973, news broke about an ongoing FBI investigation into the burglary of the Democratic National Committee's headquarters at the Watergate office complex in Washington, D.C. in 1972. Investigations and interrogations of the suspects uncovered a money trail that traced back to a Republican organization that was established to re-elect Nixon. Though initially kept under wraps by the Department of Justice, the leaking of information about the investigation by an informant that called himself "Deepthroat," to *The Washington Post* columnists Bob Woodward and Carl Bernstein, uncovered evidence that, deep within the federal government, a massive cover-up was occurring to ensure that the break-in couldn't be traced back to the White House. The uncovering of this conspiracy pushed the United States Congress to open an investigation of Nixon and his administration.

Eventually, the congressional investigation uncovered a wide abuse of power that had been ordered and controlled at the highest levels of the White House. Nixon himself was implicated in ordering the Central Intelligence Agency, the FBI and the IRS to conduct multiple illegal investigations into major political figures, many of whom were Democrats. Though the evidence hadn't proved that Nixon was ordered these actions yet, the trail became hotter when a White House employee testified that Nixon taped conversations in the Oval Office and kept those tapes for future use. Congress ordered Nixon to hand them over and, after he refused to do so, went to the Supreme Court over the issue. On July 24, 1974, the Supreme Court ruled in *United States v. Nixon* that claims of executive privilege that the White House was using to defend their refusal to hand the tapes over was invalid and ordered the tapes released.

The conversations contained on those tapes were damning. Of particular interest to Congress and the special prosecutor investigating the scandal, conversations between Nixon and his legal counsel, John Dean, literally summarized what Nixon had ordered, who carried it out and who was implicated. To make it worse, it was discovered that close to twenty minutes of conversations were erased. It was a goldmine for the prosecutor. An impeachment order was drawn up, but before it could be delivered to the White House, Nixon resigned on August 9, 1974. His successor, Vice President Gerald Ford, pardoned him of his crimes on September 8. Nixon's career, much like Vietnam, ended in failure.

Legacies and Lessons

Historians today continue to debate key aspects of the Vietnam War and its ftermath. Its effects on military, political, social and cultural history has become a source of continued theoretical advancement in history as well as in military science, sociology, anthropology and political science. As a war that caused some of the most intense years in American history, Vietnam remains both a touchy and fragile subject amongst scholars around the world. For the public, on the other hand, remembering the Vietnam War has resulted in a wide variety of commonly accepted lessons and tropes as the exact history passes from memory to legend. Yet whereas most major conflicts of the America's past have been translated into memories of victory and progress for the people, Vietnam remains one of the only wars to leave a negative imprint on the collective psyche, creating not pride and joy but regret and fear in the memories of the American public.

Within twenty years of the conflict in Vietnam, the world would see an end of the Cold War with the collapse of the Soviet Union, the rise of the United States as a leader in a unipolar world and the rise of previously marginalized nations to powerful positions in the 21st century. Though the United States entered the conflict to stop the encroachment of communism and maintain the strength of the liberal world order, their defeat in Southeast Asia did not spell disaster for that world order. It survived, and the United States continues to lead it in partnership with countries around the world. Its rival system, that of international communism, was the one that failed and was dismantled in the long run; even in those countries where communism is still the primary ideology, it has often been overshadowed by the country's desire to enter into the world order and gain the benefits from it.

For the United States, then, Vietnam was both a disaster as well as a lesson, a gift and tragedy wrapped into one. On the one hand, Americans became more careful about entering into warfare in far-away lands due to the nervousness that another Vietnam would occur. This "Vietnam Syndrome" continues to affect the nation, though the two Gulf Wars and the Afghanistan/Iraq invasion has lessened the fear slightly. On the other hand, the United States is still learning that it does not have to use military force in every spot on the globe when the rules of the international system are not being followed. Working with other states to find ways to punish transgressors has been shown to be just as effective as military engagement.

The United States Government would enter the remainder of the 1970s quickly cutting back aid to Vietnam and focusing it elsewhere. However, the money situation continued to deteriorate overtime, eventually leading to economic downturns in the latter 1970s that pushed the Democratic Party out and brought the advent of President Ronald

Reagan and the Reagan Republicans. Focus was also turned away from Southeast Asia and placed on China and the Middle East, where efforts to open up the People's Republic of China to American and Western trade succeeded after Mao's death and efforts to find a worthwhile solution to the Israeli/Palestine conflict resulted in failure.

For American servicemen who served in Vietnam, their return was also full of major problems that were consequences of the war. Due to the horrors and tragedies inherent in war, American soldiers returned home with often severe psychological conditions, which resulted in the first diagnoses and establishment of treatment plans for post-traumatic stress disorder (PTSD). Some returned home to find a society hostile against American G.I.s, but stories about violence being perpetrated against G.I.s by angry radicals doesn't have a lot of substantial evidence. The most severe problem for many of these soldiers wasn't an angry populace but severe substance abuse issues. Many of these issues were never cared for, leaving an indelible mark on the histories of thousands of Vietnam veterans. On top of that, some didn't make it home, and in one of the biggest ongoing actions since the end of the war, people continue to hunt for evidence of their family members and friends whose names do not list a date of return or a date of death. These men, either POWs or MIAs are still the subject of political campaigns across the United States.

In the end, Vietnam was both a tragedy and a classroom for the American people in learning how to exercise their immense power in a world where it is unmatched by other states. Unlike the Korean War, which has often been referred to as the "forgotten war," Vietnam is still remembered rather well in the United States, particularly due to American's comparisons of Iraq and Afghanistan to it. What is not so clearly remembered are the overwhelmingly negative results of the war that both the world and Americans are still dealing with, be it the continued fragile nature of trust in the federal government, or the ongoing ecological effects from the weapons dropped on Asian country sides, or the lack of treatment for returning veterans. Though the United States hasn't fixed all of the problems that were experienced as a result of the war, continued consciousness of those problems and a willingness to find solutions will ultimately help the American people continue to perfect the country its forefathers and veterans fought for.

Sample Test Questions

1) Remains of *Homo erectus* found in Vietnam are dated to be around _____ years old, making Vietnam one of the oldest continually habited lands in the world.

   A) 10,000
   B) 9,500,000
   C) 800,000
   D) 1,200,000

The correct answer is C:) 800,000 years old. The remains, largely dental remains, were found in caves in northern Vietnam, marking Vietnam as a potential location of the historical transition between *Homo erectus* and *Homo sapiens*.

2) The _____ culture, which developed along the Ma and Red Rivers, was the oldest culture that developed in present-day Vietnam, being a particular catalyst in the creation of the oldest kingdoms in Vietnamese history.

   A) Đông Sơn
   B) Văn Lang
   C) Âu Lạc
   D) Zhao Tuo

The correct answer is A:) Đông Sơn. This culture was a direct result of the beginning of rice cultivation, the stratification of society into key cultural and political roles, and the origin and spread of a shared culture. B and C were the two kingdoms that resulted from the political unification of disparate units that shared the common Đông Sơn culture.

3) The Vietnamese Âu Lạc kingdom was defeated by the Chinese general _____.

   A) Mao Zedong
   B) Zhao Tuo
   C) Deng Xiaoping
   D) Zhang Zuolin

The correct answer is B:) Zhao Tuo. Zhao Tuo's victory against the Âu Lạc kingdom and the collapse of the Qin Dynasty allowed him to establish the historical territory of Nanyue that was comprised of northern Vietnam and the modern day Chinese provinces of Guangdong, Guangxi, and Yunnan.

4) In _____, the Vietnamese lord Ngô Quyên achieved full independence from the Chinese Southern Han.

    A) AD 544
    B) AD 1064
    C) AD 938
    D) AD 1500

The correct answer is C:) AD 938. Ngô Quyên defeated the Southern Han at the famous Battle of Bạch Đằng River, ending the nearly 1,000 years of Chinese rule.

5) After the Battle of Bạch Đằng River, Ngô Quyên renamed the territory he won from the Chinese _____.

    A) Đại Việt
    B) Anterior Lỳ dynasty
    C) Trần
    D) Việt Quốc

The correct answer is A:) Đại Việt. Translated as "Great Viet," the land was ruled over by choices B and C. It must be remembered that Đại Việt was not the name of the ruling body, but the kingdom itself.

6) Within 500 years of the establishment of Đại Việt, _____ was introduced into Vietnam and became the dominant religion.

    A) Christianity
    B) Hinduism
    C) Shintoism
    D) Buddhism

The correct answer is D:) Buddhism. Though Christianity was later introduced through the French, Buddhism became an integral part of the history and culture of Vietnam.

7) The French were utilized religion, political support and _____ to slowly infiltrate and colonize Vietnam.

    A) Nuclear weapons
    B) Trade
    C) Religion
    D) Political intrigue

The correct answer is B:) Trade. Through the support of those they converted to Christianity, political support for the winning dynasties, and trade, they were able to weaken the Vietnamese until taking control by the end of the 19th century.

8) The most important French missionary was the Jesuit _____.

    A) Alexandre Dumas
    B) Alexis de Tocqueville
    C) Alexandre de Rhodes
    D) Louis Phillipe

The correct answer is C:) Alexandre de Rhodes. Though he was later expelled, he introduced Christianity to Vietnam and was integral in starting political partnerships between the Vietnamese and French.

9) The _____ was the failed-rebellion by the Vietnamese Nationalist Party.

    A) The Storming of the Bastille
    B) Yên Bái mutiny
    C) Boston Tea Party
    D) Huaihai Campaign

The correct answer is B:) Yên Bái mutiny. This failed action by VNQDĐ party was a direct cause of the collapse of the nationalist party in Vietnam, though nationalist ideals would be adopted into the platform of the Communist Party under Ho Chi Minh.

10) The Indochinese Communist Party was originated in the Vietnamese Revolutionary Youth League, led by _____.

   A) Ho Chi Minh
   B) Mao Zedong
   C) Chiang Kai-shek
   D) Lin Biao

The correct answer is A:) Ho Chi Minh. Though going by a different name at the time, Ho Chi Minh led the party throughout his education in Vietnam and picked up leadership duties after returning from Europe.

11) The _____ was the name of the international political program developed by Woodrow Wilson and presented at the Versailles Conference that Ho Chi Minh hoped could be used to convince the Conference to force France to grant equal rights to the Vietnamese.

   A) The Geneva Convention
   B) The Fourteen Points
   C) Liberal World Order
   D) League of Nations

The correct answer is B:) The Fourteen Points. Ho Chi Minh was particularly hopeful in the promise of Point V, which promoted the use of popular sovereignty to construct and maintain an international order that prevented war and promoted peace.

12) _____ was the important political tract written by Ho Chi Minh in which he urged his followers to use the nationalist sentiments of the Vietnamese to develop a political support network?

   A) Twelve Recommendations
   B) The Communist Manifesto
   C) The German Ideology
   D) The Little Red Book

The correct answer is A:) Twelve Recommendations. Ho knew that in order to develop a political support network that could hold-up an army fighting for independence he would have to tap into the well-established nationalist sentiments of the Vietnamese people prior to implementing a communist ideology.

13) In October 1946, a French cruiser sailing in the waters off of North Vietnam opened fire on the shore, setting off _____.

    A) World War II
    B) The First Indochina War
    C) The Vietnam War
    D) The Crimean War

The correct answer is B:) The First Indochina War. The First Indochina War (1946-1954) was fought between the French and the Vietnamese led by Ho Chi Minh. Throughout the literature, the Indochina War is often pluralized to denote two wars: the first between the French and Vietnamese, and the second between the United States and North Vietnam.

14) At _____ the Vietnamese achieved a superb victory over French forces, ultimately ending the First Indochina War.

    A) Dien Bien Phu
    B) The Battle of the Bulge
    C) The Battle of the Day River
    D) Battle of Na San

The correct answer is A:) Dien Bien Phu. In this battle, the Vietnamese, led by General Giap, were able to drag up scores of artillery weapons up the mountains around Dien Bien Phu, where they were able to cut the French off from air drops providing supplies.

15) The conference that ended the First Indochina War while simultaneously setting the stage for greater American presence in Vietnam was held in _____, Switzerland.

    A) Helsinki
    B) Moscow
    C) Beijing
    D) Geneva

The correct answer is D:) Geneva. As a result of the crushing defeat at the hands of the Vietnamese at Dien Bien Phu, the French were forced to give up their colonies in Indochina. Within a few years, the French Empire would completely disappear.

16) Vietnam was divided at the _____ parallel in the provisions of the Geneva Convention.

    A) The 38th
    B) The 17th
    C) The 21st
    D) The 19th

The correct answer is B:) The 17th. By the provisions of the Geneva Convention Treaty, Vietnam was to be divided at the 17th latitude for two years until a nationwide election would be held for the Vietnamese to choose either unification or maintenance of two different nations.

17) _____ was the name of the theory first articulated by George Kennan in the "X" article of *Foreign Affairs* that would have a driving impact on greater American presence in Vietnam.

    A) The domino theory
    B) Neorealism
    C) Containment
    D) Anti-Communism

The correct answer is C:) Containment. According to Kennan, the Soviet Union, by its very ideology, needed to spread in order to survive. To make sure that American interests were maintained and the Soviet Union didn't take more power, Kennan suggested a foreign policy plan that prevented the spread of Soviet Communism abroad, essentially "containing" the USSR to Russia and East Europe.

18) _____ became the president of South Vietnam and an ally to the United States against the North Vietnamese.

    A) Bao Dai
    B) Mao Zedong
    C) Ngo Dinh Diem
    D) Deng Xiaoping

The correct answer is C:) Ngo Dinh Diem. Diem would become the United States' ally in Vietnam, though his inadequacies would continue to test both the United States' and Vietnamese people's patience.

19) The _____ administration was the first to begin providing sustained and large-scale economic and military aid to South Vietnam in the 1950s.

   A) The Eisenhower Administration
   B) The Roosevelt Administration
   C) The Kennedy Administration
   D) The Nixon Administration

The correct answer is A:) The Eisenhower Administration. Eisenhower's foreign policy revolved primarily on providing military and economic aid to states around the world facing off against communist forces. As a leading general of World War II, Eisenhower was very careful in relying too heavily on the armed forces, opting instead to conduct foreign policy through both aid packages and covert action.

20) The Eisenhower Administration sent the first aid package worth $216 million to the South Vietnamese Government in _____ .

   A) 1954
   B) 1955
   C) 1960
   D) 1957

The correct answer is B:) 1955. An eventful time during the Cold War, 1955 was the year that the East/West divide between the Soviet Union and the United States hardened into its commonly known version.

21) Ngo Dinh Diem essentially overthrew _____ through a national referendum on October 23, 1955?

   A) Ho Chi Minh
   B) Mao Zedong
   C) Bao Dai
   D) Chiang Kai-Shek

The correct answer is C:) Bao Dai. Bao Dai was the emperor prior to the outbreak of World War II. After the Japanese were defeated, he was reinstated as the puppet emperor by the French and ultimately overthrown by Diem in 1955.

22) Three days after ousting Bao Dai on October 23, 1955, Diem _____.

    A) Proclaimed the creation of the Republic of Vietnam
    B) Went to Disney World
    C) Committed suicide
    D) Invaded North Vietnam

The correct answer is A:) He proclaimed the creation of the Republic of Vietnam. In the same proclamation, he named himself president, beginning a despotic rule that bring trouble both to South Vietnam and the United States.

23) The _____ was first articulated by Secretary of State John Foster Dulles and called for heightened aid to states fighting communism, for fear that once they collapsed, the neighboring state would as well.

    A) Containment Theory
    B) Classical Realism
    C) Domino Theory
    D) Mutual Assured Destruction

The correct answer is C:) Domino Theory. The domino theory is exactly what it sounds like: if one state fell to communism, the neighboring state would fall as well, like the next domino in the set. Both the domino theory and containment theory called for U.S. commitment, in the form of economic and military aid, to states fighting communism to ensure that it did not spread across the globe.

24) Diem began fighting the growing insurgency in the South in _____, ultimately pushing Ho Chi Minh and the Viet Minh to begin supporting the insurgents more.

    A) 1959
    B) 1942
    C) 1948
    D) 1951

The correct answer is A:) 1959. In particular, January 1959. As stated in the chapter, though resistance movements were relatively spread out and actions against the South Vietnamese Government sporadic, they began to unify at the same time that Diem announced the presence of an insurgency movement. It was then, after several years of pleading with the North to send aid, that Ho Chi Minh and the Viet Minh finally began to support the insurgents.

25) On December 20, 1960, the insurgent movements, now receiving aid from the North to fight Diem's South Vietnamese Government, unified to form the
_____.

    A) The People's Army of Vietnam
    B) The Peasant's Army of Vietnam
    C) The Viet Cong
    D) The Viet Minh

The correct answer is C:) The Viet Cong. The VC would remain the military arm of Northern actions prior to the entrance of the United States into the war. Only during the period that American efforts against the North Vietnamese ramped up would the North Vietnamese Army get more involved.

26) _____ was the name of the counterinsurgency program first developed by South Vietnam and the United States in 1962.

    A) The Hearts and Minds Campaign
    B) The Strategic Hamlet Program
    C) The Great Red March
    D) Operation Jungle Storm

The correct answer is B:) The Strategic Hamlet Program. This counterinsurgency plan called for the creation of "protected hamlets" that would be shielded from Viet Cong control and strengthened by American and South Vietnamese aid.

27) _____ were a series of protests that broke out in reaction to Diem's pro-Catholic policies in 1963.

    A) The Occupy Movement
    B) The Civil Rights Movement
    C) The Buddhist Crisis
    D) The Anti-Catholic March

The correct answer is C:) The Buddhist Crisis. Much of Diem's political program was aimed at benefiting Catholics and South Vietnamese nationalists, marginalizing the Buddhist majority of the country. This resulted in the outbreak of massive protests—led largely by Buddhist monks—that threatened the legitimacy of the Diem regime.

28) The Battle of _____ in January 1963 exemplified the continued weakness of the South Vietnamese Army.

    A) Dien Bien Phu
    B) Battle of Ap Bac
    C) Battle of Saigon
    D) The Tet Offensive

The correct answer is B:) Battle of Ap Bac. Though the South Vietnamese Army continued to operate with large levels of support from the American government, they continued to lose in battle. By 1963, the North Vietnamese Army had begun to enter the conflict, joining forces with the Viet Cong to fight largely conventional battles which they won.

29) The coup and assassination of Ngo Dinh Diem occurred on November 2, _____.

    A) 1963
    B) 1960
    C) 1951
    D) 1958

The correct answer is A:) 1963. On November 2, South Vietnamese military officials, fed up with the tyrannical rule of Diem and his brother (who was the chief of the secret police), launched an internal coup that removed both from power. Within hours, they executed Diem and his brother.

30) Following the Diem coup, South Vietnam experienced _____ for the next several years.

    A) Business continued as usual
    B) Bao Dai was returned to the throne
    C) Large-scale political instability
    D) Restrictions on political activities tightened

The correct answer is C:) Large-scale political instability. Within the next three years, a series of military coups would replace each regime with another as a power struggle continued.

31) President John F Kennedy was succeeded by _____ after he was assassinated on November 22, 1963.

    A) Dwight Eisenhower
    B) Henry Kissinger
    C) Richard Nixon
    D) Lyndon Baines Johnson

The correct answer is D:) Lyndon Baines Johnson. Sworn in on Air Force One mere hours after Kennedy's assassination, his quick inauguration is forever cemented in history through the photograph showing him taking the oath of office next to Jackie Kennedy, former First Lady, who still wears the clothes she was in when her husband was shot sitting next to her.

32) The _____ was the name of Johnson's domestic legislative program.

    A) New Frontier
    B) Great Society
    C) New Deal
    D) A New Hope

The correct answer is B:) Great Society. Aimed to implement Kennedy's vision of civil rights, infrastructural, and economic legislation, the Great Society legislative package flew through Congress, who approved it mere months after Johnson announced it.

33) The _____ were a series of events that pushed Congress to grant President Johnson the ability to order military actions in Vietnam.

    A) The North Vietnamese invaded the South
    B) The Gulf of Tonkin Incidents
    C) The fall of Saigon
    D) The agreement between North Vietnam and China to join forces

The correct answer is B:) The Gulf of Tonkin Incidents. Occurring on August 2 and 4, 1964 when two Navy destroyers were apparently fired upon by North Vietnamese forces from the shore in the Gulf of Tonkin, the Gulf of Tonkin Incident would be uncovered as a lie by the Pentagon Papers.

34) Johnson defeated _____ in the 1964 Presidential elections

    A) Barry Goldwater
    B) Richard Nixon
    C) Hubert Humphrey
    D) Al Gore

The correct answer is A:) Barry Goldwater. Goldwater, originally from Arizona, ran on a conservative platform that would be the foundation for modern Republican conservatism.

35) _____ was name of the air operation called that occurred between March 1965 and October 1968?

    A) Operation Big Boom
    B) Operation Horizon
    C) Operation Rolling Thunder
    D) Operation Overlord

The correct answer is C:) Operation Rolling Thunder. A massive bombing campaign, Operation Rolling Thunder was aimed at putting increased military pressure on the North Vietnamese by bombing key economic and industrial centers and to shut down the Ho Chi Minh Trail.

36) The first 3,500 Marines sent to Vietnam, the beginning of the troop surge that would mark the beginning of full-scale American participation in the war occurred in _____.

    A) March 1965
    B) April 1963
    C) June 1970
    D) December 1971

The correct answer is A:) March 1965. The deployment of 3,500 Marines were the first official ground units sent over. Their original mission was defensive: guard the perimeter of American and South Vietnamese air fields from Viet Cong attacks.

37) _____ was the commander of American forces in Vietnam until 1968.

    A) Dwight Eisenhower
    B) Douglas MacArthur
    C) Ulysses S Grant
    D) William Westmoreland

The correct answer is D:) William Westmoreland. Westmoreland's primary concern was the morale of the South Vietnamese Army (ARVN) so he called for a three-phased plan that called for a greater number of troops to be placed on an offensive footing in Vietnam.

38) Westmoreland's plan was approved by Johnson to increase ground troop numbers in _____.

    A) July 1965
    B) March 1962
    C) February 1970
    D) August 1969

The correct answer is A:) July 1965. Westmoreland, in his initial proposal, was confident that the war would end within two years when the military superiority of the United States stripped the will to fight from the North Vietnamese.

39) The series of paths, routes and tunnels that the North Vietnamese used to funnel supplies and troops to the Viet Cong was called _____.

    A) The Southern Trail
    B) The Northern Trail
    C) The Ho Chi Minh Trail
    D) The Karl Marx Trail

The correct answer is C:) The Ho Chi Minh Trail. The trail would remain central to the North's war strategy throughout the war.

40) Westmoreland was forced to undertake _____ warfare after the North Vietnamese refused to fold and continued fighting through 1966?

    A) Siege
    B) Attrition
    C) Offensive
    D) Civil

The correct answer is B:) Attrition. Though closely related to siege warfare in that they both aimed for the same goal, attrition warfare aimed to fight the North Vietnamese until they lost their will to fight.

41) _____ was the measurement of success used by the Pentagon while Westmoreland was commander.

    A) Territory conquered
    B) Enemy commanders captured
    C) Body count
    D) Money gained

The correct answer is C:) Body count. This statistically-driven measurement was aimed at justifying the war to the American public and government by detailing how many of the enemy were killed or captured. The problem with the method was that the numbers reported were often way off the mark in accuracy, leading to the belief that the war was going well.

42) The type of bombing undertaken by the United States Air Force was called _____.

    A) Saturation bombing
    B) Tactical bombing
    C) Strategic bombing
    D) Defensive bombing

The correct answer is A:) Saturation bombing. Also known as "carpet bombing," saturation bombing is an aerial tactic in which the attacker drops tons of explosives on both population centers and unpopulated areas to destroy as much of the population, infrastructure, industry and agriculture of the enemy as possible.

43) After a coup in 1965 and political maneuvering in 1967, _____ took over as ruler of South Vietnam until 1975.

    A) Bao Dai
    B) Nguyen Cao Ky
    C) Nguyen Van Thieu
    D) Deng Xiaoping

The correct answer is C:) Nguyen Van Thieu. Using crafty political maneuvers, he was able to remove his partner, Nguyen Cao Ky, from power after the two of them completed the final coup in 1965.

44) _____ was the name given by soldiers to the type of conventional warfare fought with clear fronts and labeled enemy.

    A) Warfare
    B) The Good War
    C) The Regular War
    D) The War We Trained For

The correct answer is B:) The Good War. The Vietnam War, fought against guerrilla elements who attacked then disappeared into the jungle and villages, was one that had a severe impact on the psyche of the American soldier. When fighting against an enemy wearing a uniform at a front that would move with each victory and defeat the soldier remained psychologically more ready and understanding. It should be noted that the soldiers did not mean that there was anything "good" about war, but that it was better understood and it was what they trained for.

45) _____ was a major battle in the first years of war that soldiers would consider part of the "good war."

    A) Dien Bien Phu
    B) Battle of Silver Lake
    C) Battle of Ia Drang
    D) Battle of Midway

The correct answer is C:) The Battle of Ia Drang. One of the first major conventional battles between US and North Vietnamese forces, the battle occurred in the Ia Drang Valley in the Central Highlands of South Vietnam between November 14 and 18, 1965.

46) The _____ division of the United States Army was sent into the Ia Drang Valley to search for and destroy enemy forces.

    A) The 1st Cavalry Division
    B) The 7th Cavalry Division
    C) The 1st Infantry Division
    D) The 29th Infantry Division

The correct answer is A:) The 1st Cavalry Division. Though the 7th Cavalry Division (B) would be sent in after the battle was underway to reinforce the 1st, the 3rd Brigade of the 1st Cavalry Division were the first to find and enter into combat against the North Vietnamese Army in Ia Drang.

47) _____ was the Secretary of Defense throughout the Johnson Administration.

    A) Robert Gates
    B) Colin Powell
    C) Robert McNamara
    D) Robert Kennedy

The correct answer is C:) Robert McNamara. McNamara, a former executive of the Ford Motor Company, served as Defense Secretary for the Kennedy and Johnson Administrations, eventually leaving office as the American public grew to oppose the war more-and-more.

48) Southern Democrats were called _____ in the 1960s.

    A) SoDems
    B) Arch-Democrats
    C) Core Democrats
    D) Dixiecrats

The correct answer is D:) Dixiecrats. A mixture of "Dixie," a popular nickname for the Southern United States, and "-crat" the end of "democrat" the Dixiecrats helped push Johnson's Great Society legislative program through Congress.

49) _____ and _____ were two federal laws passed during the Johnson Administration that are considered the two crowning achievements of his Great Society program.

    A) The Equal Rights Act and Johnson Act
    B) The Civil Rights Act and Voting Rights Act
    C) The Civil Rights Act and the Johnson Act
    D) The Equal Rights Act and Voting Rights Act

The correct answer is B:) The Civil Rights Act and Voting Rights Act. Both acts, of 1964 and 1965, respectively, were breakthrough victories for both the Johnson Administration and the Civil Rights Movement.

50) A massive riot broke out in the African-American community in 1964 in _____.

    A) Chicago
    B) Houston
    C) Miami
    D) Los Angeles

The correct answer is D:) Los Angeles. Occurring primarily in the African-American neighborhood Watts neighborhood, the riot resulted from accusations of police brutality between August 11 and 16, 1965.

51) _____ was the first major protest of the modern Civil Rights Movement.

    A) The Montgomery Bus Boycott
    B) The Selma March
    C) The Freedom Riders
    D) The Anti-Discrimination March

The correct answer is A:) The Montgomery Bus Boycott. The Boycott started after Rosa Parks, an African-American woman, was kicked off of a bus for refusing to give up her seat. A politically planned act, the boycott nonetheless brought together various protest groups to join in in Montgomery.

52) The Supreme Court ruling _____ ruled that the "separate but equal" doctrine was unconstitutional, thus eliminating segregation in schools and public places.

    A) *Loving v. Virginia*
    B) *Roe v. Wade*
    C) *Brown v. Board of Education*
    D) *McCullough v. Maryland*

The correct answer is C:) *Brown v. Board of Education*. This historical ruling by the Supreme Court set the stage for the Civil Rights Movement to successfully petition the desegregation efforts of the federal government under Johnson.

53) The most well-known and visible leader of the Civil Rights Movement was

_____.

    A) Angela Davis
    B) Malcolm X
    C) Rosa Parks
    D) Martin Luther King Jr.

The correct answer is D:) Martin Luther King Jr. Though all of the choices were leaders of the Civil Rights Movement, and important in their own right, the individual who most considered the leader, and is the most remembered as such, was King.

54) With the advent of new media devices, the Vietnam War became known as the

_____.

    A) The Telegram War
    B) The Television War
    C) The Radio War
    D) The DVD War

The correct answer is B:) The Television War. Nicknamed this because of the growing popularity of television sets in American homes, coupled with the influx of television news reporters into battlefields, the combat of the Vietnam War was broadcast across million televisions on the nightly news, leading to a growth in public awareness of the details of the war.

55) _____ was the name of the first major anti-war group.

  A) Students for a Democratic Society
  B) Students Against the War
  C) Campus Communists
  D) Campus Anti-War Movement

The correct answer is A:) Students for a Democratic Society (SDS). Founded in the early 1960s, the organization was founded and active on college campuses across the nation, though the most active were on the University of California, Berkeley and University of Michigan campuses.

56) The name of the intellectual movement that emerged from opposition movements on college campuses across the nation is called the _____.

  A) The Left
  B) The Far Left
  C) The American Communists
  D) The New Left

The correct answer is D:) The New Left. The New Left was an intellectual and political movement that encompassed a broad range of radical ideas, most notably critical Marxism.

57) The name of the photographer whose photographs of the My Lai Massacre ignited further opposition to the war when they were printed in the *Cleveland Plain-Dealer* was _____.

  A) John Fremont
  B) Ronald Haeberle
  C) Allen Baez
  D) Robert Bly

The correct answer is B) Ronald Haeberle. Haeberle's photographs further consolidated the already-extant opposition movement against the war as well as bringing new members of the American public into the fold against the war.

58) _____ was the name given to the countercultural movement that developed in the 1960s in San Francisco and New York that developed their own music, separate communities and experiment in drug usage.

   A) The Hipsters
   B) The Yuppies
   C) The Hippies
   D) The Beats

The correct answer is C:) The Hippies. The Hippies formed largely in the Haight-Ashbury district of San Francisco, developing new values, identities and interests separate from the American culture.

59) An umbrella term often used by historians studying the 1960s to describe any social movement that opposed mainstream society and culture is the _____ movement.

   A) Countercultural
   B) Student Protest
   C) Civil Rights
   D) Democratic Surge

The correct answer is A:) Countercultural. This term, while often thrown around in discussions of the period, refers to a broad range of social movements that sprung up in the United States in the 1960s. Though not all referring to anti-war groups, the Vietnam War and the culture it created in the United States aided in its rise.

60) At the height of the Vietnam War the _____ was created when the reports being delivered during the news became so radically different from the official record of how the war was going that doubt in the veracity of President Johnson's statements came into the public discourse.

   A) Congressional Dissent
   B) Credibility Gap
   C) Statistical anomaly
   D) Institutional Doubt

The correct answer is B:) Credibility Gap. The credibility gap occurred when the contradictions in stories became increasingly evident. As time went on and the war continued, American citizens began to question whether Johnson was telling the truth about the war. As they learned within the next few years, not only had he been continually lying, but every president before him down to Truman had lied as well.

61) The Tet Offensive occurred on the Vietnamese _____, an opportune time as the South Vietnamese and American's guard would be down due to celebrations.

A) Harvest Day
B) Remembrance Day
C) New Year's Day
D) Fall Equinox

The correct answer is C:) New Year's Day. The Tet holiday was an important one for the South Vietnamese Buddhist population, who used it as a day of celebration and remembrance. When the attack occurred, most were partaking in specific holiday activities and were thus taken by surprise.

62) In order to draw the attention of the American forces away from the primary target sites for the Tet Offensive, General Giap and the North Vietnamese launched an attack on the Marine base at _____ on January 21, 1968.

A) Saigon
B) Ia Drang
C) Hanoi
D) Khe Sanh

The correct answer is D:) Khe Sanh. At the battle for Khe Sanh, American troops fought and undertook a valiant defense against Viet Cong and North Vietnamese forces. An important battle in its own right, it is overshadowed by the Tet Offensive that occurred ten days later, particularly as it was nothing more than a diversion to draw as many American military personnel as possible away from the primary targets.

63) The Tet Offensive occurred on _____.

A) January 30, 1968
B) February 8, 1970
C) May 2, 1965
D) April 24, 1969

The correct answer is A:) January 30, 1968. As related in the chapter, the attack began ten days prior to this launch and, just as important, the offensive stretched for months after this initial attack, lasting largely until September 1968.

64) After Secretary of Defense Robert McNamara stepped down following the Tet Offensive, his replacement _____ began to publicly and within cabinet meetings campaign to withdraw American forces from Vietnam.

A) Henry Kissinger
B) Clark Clifford
C) Harry Reid
D) Douglas MacArthur

The correct answer is B:) Clark Clifford. Clifford had been one of McNamara's lieutenants throughout his tenure as Secretary of Defense. By the time the Tet Offensive occurred, Clifford began understanding that the war couldn't be won, pushing him to being campaigning to withdraw American forces from Indochina.

65) After Johnson announced that he would not seek reelection in 1968, the Democrats began fierce infighting, ultimately helping _____ win the 1968 presidential election.

A) Barry Goldwater
B) Ronald Reagan
C) Richard Nixon
D) Gerald Ford

The correct answer is C:) Richard Nixon. Nixon had been the Republican candidate for president in 1960, where he was defeated by John F. Kennedy and, prior to that, was vice president under Eisenhower. Nixon had made his name back in the early 1950s as a particularly stringent supporter and worker for Joseph McCarthy, whose Communist witch hunts constituted the Red Scare of the 1950s.

66) At the Democratic National Convention in _____, protestors clashed with police, creating visions of anarchy on the steps of the convention.

A) New York
B) Los Angeles
C) Denver
D) Chicago

The correct answer is D:) Chicago. Chicago's mayor, Richard Daley, wanted to have his city presentable to the visiting political elite. When anti-war protesters began congregating in a nearby park, he ordered the police to stop them from marching. After several arrests, violence broke out, eventually culminating in a riot.

67) The _____, held on October 15 and November 15, 1969, became the largest anti-war protest during the Vietnam War, ultimately becoming one of the largest protests in American history.

    A) Stop War Now! Campaign
    B) Moratorium to End the War in Vietnam
    C) The Workers' Strike
    D) Protest Against Nixon

The correct answer is B:) Moratorium to End the War in Vietnam. Originally intended to be a nationwide strike but toned down to include more people, the anti-war march drew in hundreds of thousands of people, including many ordinary, non-radical American citizens who were nonetheless opposed to the war.

68) In November 1968, the public was alerted to a massacre that had been committed by American soldiers at _____.

    A) Hanoi
    B) Saigon
    C) My Lai
    D) Shanghai

The correct answer is C:) My Lai. My Lai was one of two hamlets of a larger village that, according to intelligence reports, had been sheltering Viet Cong guerrillas. After a particularly violent war, the unit set in ultimately rounded the villagers up and began murdering, torturing, and raping them until an American helicopter pilot landed his craft between fleeing villagers and chasing soldiers, threatening the troops that he would fire upon them if they did not stop.

69) On May 4, 1970, students at _____ University in Ohio were fired upon by national guardsmen who were called in to stop protests on the campus.

    A) Ohio State
    B) Ohio
    C) Case Western Reserve
    D) Kent State

The correct answer is D:) Kent State. The days leading up to the May 4th event had been filled with numerous protests and violence between students and police officers. The guardsmen that fired on the students were mostly in the same age group, and reasons for them firing have remained unknown.

70) In February 1971, former Defense Department contractor _____ leaked 43 volumes of a classified Pentagon report on the Vietnam War to reporters at *The New York Times* and *The Washington Post.*

   A) Daniel Ellsberg
   B) Howard Zinn
   C) Edward Snowden
   D) Bradley Manning

The correct answer is A:) Daniel Ellsberg. The 43-volume report became known as the "Pentagon Papers" and ultimately told the story that American presidents since Truman had lied to the American public about the levels of their involvement in Vietnam.

71) Nixon's war plan for Vietnam, which he called _____, called for the supplying and training of South Vietnamese troops to fight the North on their own with less help from American ground troops.

   A) The Good Fight
   B) Vietnamization
   C) Southern Strengthening
   D) Southern Support

The correct answer is B:) Vietnamization. The ultimate goal of this plan was to have the majority of American military personnel stationed in Vietnam home by the Spring of 1971.

72) In an attempt to spread the _____ to neighboring Cambodia and Laos, the North Vietnamese were instrumental in spreading the war into these states as well.

   A) United States Military
   B) Viet Cong
   C) Ho Chi Minh Trail
   D) North Vietnamese Army

The correct answer is C:) Ho Chi Minh Trail. The network of supply routes that extended from North Vietnam to the South were used to provide arms, material, and reinforcements to Viet Cong and North Vietnamese Army personnel. In an attempt to provide needed resources to the units operating along the border regions of South Vietnam, the North attempted to extend the Trail into both Cambodia and Laos.

73) In Operation _____, Nixon ordered the beginning of a bombing campaign against Communist targets in Cambodian territory.

    A) Jungle Storm
    B) Menu
    C) Rolling Thunder
    D) Heavy Rain

The correct answer is B:) Menu. Beginning as a bombing campaign against Communist targets, American and North Vietnamese actions in Cambodia exacerbated an already-extant Cambodian domestic struggle between forces loyal to the United States and the Communist-aligned Khmer Rouge. As a result of the bombing campaign, the North invaded to provide aid to the Khmer Rouge, forcing the United States and South Vietnam to enter as well.

74) In July and October 1971, Nixon's national security advisor _____, an important architect of Nixon's foreign policy and Vietnamization, met with Chinese leaders to set up a meeting between Nixon and Chairman Mao.

    A) Clark Clifford
    B) Colin Powell
    C) Robert Gates
    D) Henry Kissinger

The correct answer is D:) Henry Kissinger. Kissinger, a former professor of political science and history at Harvard, was instrumental in establishing a realist framework for American foreign policy beginning in the 1970s. His work in negotiations led to an opening of diplomatic communications and agreements with the Soviet Union and China.

75) Prior to his visit to the People's Republic of China, Kissinger was instrumental in establishing the groundwork for Nixon's negotiations with the Soviet Union to create _____, a term that refers to the opening of better communications and slightly better relations.

A) Détente
B) Containment
C) Formalization
D) Deterrence

The correct answer is A:) Détente. Détente, a French word meaning "relaxation" is essentially the relaxing of strained relations in any political situation. In this case, the term refers to the relaxation of tensions between the USSR and United States that began in 1969.

76) In February 1972, President Nixon visited and toured China where, after discussions with Chinese leadership, they came to an agreement on a peaceful settlement of _____, a diplomatic disagreement that had been holding back all other negotiations.

A) Mongolia
B) Japan
C) Taiwan
D) South China Sea

The correct answer is C:) Taiwan. Following the Communist victory in China in 1949, nationalist forces loyal to former-president Chiang Kai-Shek fled to Taiwan. Within a year, the Korean War broke out which allowed the United States to place to Navy's Seventh Fleet in the Taiwan Strait between the two belligerents. This stopped any possibility of either side attack the other, but also led to a particularly sticky-point of contention between the PRC and US. After this was settled, better negotiation terms could be opened for ending the war in Vietnam.

77) As a result of his use of television crews and news media outlets to publicize his trip to China, Nixon was able to win the _____ election with an over-whelming number of votes.

    A) 1972
    B) 1973
    C) 1974
    D) 1976

The correct answer is A:) 1972. To add to his popularity and to seal his victory, Nixon announced, a month prior to the elections, that talks had begun between the United States and China to bring the North and South Vietnamese to the table to discuss peace.

78) On _____, Nixon announced the end of hostilities to the American public.

    A) March 10, 1980
    B) August 1, 1960
    C) January 15, 1973
    D) May 2, 1965

The correct answer is C:) January 15, 1973. The cease-fire agreement made between the belligerents went into effect on January 27, 1973.

79) According to the agreements, a cease-fire period and a _____ day window were created to withdraw American forces from Vietnam.

    A) 100
    B) 60
    C) 40
    D) 10

The correct answer is B:) 60. Essentially two months to withdraw their forces, the Americans left a parting gift for the South Vietnamese in the form of military supplies.

80) Officially titled "The Agreement on Ending the War and Restoring the Peace in Vietnam," the treaty between the belligerents became known as the _____.

A) Geneva Convention
B) Helsinki Accords
C) Camp David Accords
D) Paris Peace Accords

The correct answer is D:) Paris Peace Accords. The agreement only ended direct American involvement in Vietnam, but within months of its signing, hostilities started again between the North and South Vietnamese.

81) Beginning in 1975, North Vietnam, after experiencing a series of defeats against the South who used American supplies and armaments to push the Viet Cong and North Vietnamese towards the border, began the _____, an offensive unmatched in ferocity and success in the rest of the war for the North Vietnamese.

A) Tet Offensive
B) Summer Rush
C) Great Spring Offensive
D) Great Southern Push

The correct answer is C:) Great Spring Offensive. The offensive was the culmination and final push of North Vietnam's efforts to take control of and unify Vietnam.

82) On _____, after a particularly fierce battle as the South Vietnamese Army defended the city, Saigon and the Republic of South Vietnam fell.

A) April 30, 1975
B) May 2, 1968
C) August 1, 1965
D) December 20, 1970

The correct answer is A:) April 30, 1975. The fall of Saigon became particularly famous to the air lift the American military was forced to undertake, landing helicopters on skyscrapers' roofs in Saigon to evacuate American personnel and a lucky few South Vietnamese citizens.

83) With the passage of the _____, Congress removed the president's power to place American troops into combat without approval of Congress, a law that has been broken in numerous occasions since its passage.

   A) Great Society Act
   B) Anti-War Act
   C) War Powers Act
   D) Gulf of Tonkin Resolutions

The correct answer is C:) War Powers Act. Though giving the American President the ability to exercise his executive prerogatives of defending the United States, prior-Congressional approval for any large-scale deployment of American troops was required.

84) In 1972, a group of burglars was caught breaking into the headquarters of the _____ at the Watergate office complex in Washington.

   A) Democratic National Committee
   B) Rand Corporation
   C) FBI Washington Field Office
   D) Committee to Re-elect the President

The correct answer is A:) Democratic National Committee. Essentially the home office of the Democratic Party's campaign in the 1972 elections, the office in Watergate was supposedly well-guarded, but the burglars were caught only after a witness saw the burglars breaking in and alerted the police.

85) After interrogating the burglars, FBI agents and local police discovered a _____ that seemingly led back to the White House.

   A) Trail of Blood
   B) Money Trail
   C) Employment Record
   D) Wire

The correct answer is B:) Money Trail. The money paid to the burglars was traced back to a slush fund operated by a Republican campaign coordinating organization called the Committee to Re-elect the President. In an ironic twist, the acronym of the organization was CREEP, a fitting word for the burglars.

86) The investigation into ties between the burglars and key White House figures was initially _____.

    A) Tossed out
    B) Given to Congress to conduct their own investigation
    C) Covered up
    D) Announced on the nightly news

The correct answer is C:) Covered up. Due to the findings that the chain of command that ordered the break in implicated leadership of the Federal Bureau of Investigation and Department of Justice, the findings were initially covered up in an attempt to stop the investigation.

87) Even though there were official attempts to cover-up the investigation and its findings, a high level FBI informant who went by the nom de guerre _____.

    A) Frost
    B) Deepthroat
    C) Forger
    D) Strongman

The correct answer is B:) Deepthroat. Deepthroat's identity would remain secret for 31 years after the break-in and subsequent investigation, until a family attorney announced that former FBI Associate Director Mark Felt was Deepthroat in 2005.

88) Deepthroat's information, leaked to *The Washington Post* columnists _____ and _____, alerted the journalists to a cover-up that did not end with the FBI, but was directed at higher levels by the White House.

    A) Bob Bernstein and Carl Woodward
    B) Bob Woodward and Carl Bernstein
    C) Jack Stein and Jack Frost
    D) E. Howard Hunt and Carl Bernstein

The correct answer is B:) Bob Woodward and Carl Bernstein. Though both became famous for their investigative journalism that alerted the American public to a massive cover-up, and led Congress to open investigations into the matter, they would become legend through the movie *All the President's Men*.

89) After a Congressional special prosecutor investigation discovered evidence of _____ that recorded the conversations in the Oval Office, Nixon was ordered to turn them over.

   A) Video tapes
   B) Journal articles
   C) Official records
   D) Audio tapes

The correct answer is D:) Audio tapes. According to a high-ranking White House employee and counselor to Nixon, Nixon recorded all conversations that occurred in the White House, which included a conversation that essentially provided a smoking gun that Nixon ordered the break-in.

90) After refusing to turn over the audio tapes, Congress took Nixon to court, which culminated in the July 24, 1974 ruling in _____ that ordered Nixon to turn over the tapes.

   A) *Loving v. Virginia*
   B) *Congress v. Presidential Administration*
   C) *United States v. Nixon*
   D) *Madison v. Marbury*

The correct answer is C:) *United States v. Nixon*. In this ruling, the Supreme Court struck down Nixon's defense that executive privilege allowed him to refuse to turn over the audio tapes.

91) The series of investigations that culminated in Nixon's resignation became known as the _____.

   A) Nixon Impeachment
   B) Audio Tapes Leak
   C) Republican Break-in
   D) Watergate Scandal

The correct answer is D:) Watergate Scandal. The scandal became so immense in American politics and society that the suffix "-gate" is now often applied to modern scandals, i.e. "Benghazi-gate," "Deflate-gate," etc.

92) Nixon, knowing that the conversations contained on the audio tapes would force his removal from office, resigned on _____.

    A) August 9, 1974
    B) July 24, 1974
    C) June 1, 1972
    D) April 11, 1970

The correct answer is A) August 9, 1974. The previous day, impeachment orders against the President were drawn up and submitted to Congress. Knowing that the evidence on those tapes would cause him to lose the impeachment trial, Nixon opted instead to resign.

93) After his resignation, Nixon was succeeded by _____, his vice president.

    A) Henry Kissinger
    B) Clark Clifford
    C) Gerald Ford
    D) George H.W. Bush

The correct answer is C:) Gerald Ford. Prior to becoming Nixon's Vice President, Ford was a representative from Michigan, a state he became popular in after being a football star at the University of Michigan.

94) On _____ Gerald Ford pardoned Nixon, claiming that in order to move forward, the charges against Nixon had to be dropped.

    A) August 9, 1974
    B) September 8, 1974
    C) December 31, 1970
    D) May 1, 1973

The correct answer is B:) September 8, 1974. The pardon, though causing political ripples for the Ford Administration essentially ended the debacle. However, the White House officials that had worked for Nixon and carried out the orders went unpardoned, charged with their offenses from which most received prison sentences.

95) A peculiar legacy of the Vietnam War has become known as _____, which describes the stances of the American public against getting involved in long, drawn-out wars for fear of losing like they did in Vietnam.

    A) Anti-War Sentiment
    B) Isolationism
    C) Vietnam Syndrome
    D) Military Doubt

The correct answer is C:) Vietnam Syndrome. Vietnam Syndrome is a general aversion by the American public to enter warfare. Though thought to have ended with the two Gulf Wars, the invasion and war in Afghanistan and Iraq saw a reemergence of Vietnam Syndrome symptoms in the American public.

96) During the Vietnam War and its aftermath, psychologists began to first diagnose soldiers with _____, a mental disorder that began to be further explored and treated beginning in the 1970s.

    A) Shell shock
    B) Post-Traumatic Stress Disorder
    C) Split Personality Disorder
    D) Multiple Personality Disorder

The correct answer is B:) Post-Traumatic Stress Disorder. Shortened to its more commonly known acronym PTSD, the symptoms of Post-Traumatic Stress Disorder had variably been called Shell shock, Combat Stress Fatigue and Battle Fatigue and include disturbing thoughts, feelings, or dreams related to the events experienced in combat that severely affected the lives and well-being of veterans.

97) After the death of Chairman Mao, _____ opened up continued communications with the United States and ultimately began to join the liberal world order in the 1970s.

    A) Taiwan
    B) Japan
    C) China
    D) Mongolia

The correct answer is C:) China. Led by Deng Xiaoping, China began to move away from its hardline Communist policies that had marked the country throughout Mao's reign. Though maintaining a Communistic and authoritarian rule of government, China was able to create a market economy in China beginning in the 1970s ultimately leading to the explosive growth seen in the country's economy in the 21st century.

98) After cutting back economic aid to the Vietnamese after the fall of Saigon, the economic situation in the United States began to deteriorate and only turned around during the Republican presidency of _____ in the 1980s.

A) Ronald Reagan
B) Richard Nixon
C) George H.W. Bush
D) Bill Clinton

The correct answer is A:) Ronald Reagan. Reagan's Republican Administration was the culmination of the Goldwater Conservatism that had begun in the 1960s.

99) A continued campaign searching for _____ and _____ from Vietnam has continued to operate well into the 21st century.

A) Good and Bad Deeds
B) Violence and Massacres
C) POWs and MIAs
D) Failures and Successes

The correct answer is C:) POWs and MIAs. Acronyms standing for "Prisoner of War" and "Missing in Action," these soldiers that never returned home remain on the minds of the American public, who have continued to search for clues on what happened to these missing soldiers.

100) The more recent military campaigns in _____ and _____ have often been compared to Vietnam, giving particular relevance to remembering the War.

A) Lebanon and Granawda
B) Greece and Ukraine
C) Afghanistan and Iraq
D) Costa Rica and Puerto Rico

The correct answer is C:) Afghanistan and Iraq. The nature of these two wars, particularly after the devolved into insurgencies that forced the war to draw out longer than the proposed short-term that was initially told to the public has drawn many comparisons with the Vietnam War.

Test Taking Strategies

Here are some test-taking strategies that are specific to this test and to other DSST tests in general:

- Keep your eyes on the time. Pay attention to how much time you have left.
- Read the entire question and read all the answers. Many questions are not as hard to answer as they may seem. Sometimes, a difficult sounding question really only is asking you how to read an accompanying chart. Chart and graph questions are on most DANTES/DSST tests and should be an easy free point.
- If you don't know the answer immediately, the new computer-based testing lets you mark questions and come back to them later if you have time.
- Read the wording carefully. Some words can give you hints to the right answer. There are no exceptions to an answer when there are words in the question such as always, all or none. If one of the answer choices includes most or some of the right answers, but not all, then that is not the answer. Here is an example:

    The primary colors include all of the following:
    A) Red, Yellow, Blue, Green
    B) Red, Green, Yellow
    C) Red, Orange, Yellow
    D) Red, Yellow, Blue

    Although item A includes all the right answers, it also includes an incorrect answer, making it incorrect. If you didn't read it carefully, were in a hurry, or didn't know the material well, you might fall for this.

- Make a guess on a question that you do not know the answer to. There is no penalty for an incorrect answer. Eliminate the answer choices that you know are incorrect. For example, this will let your guess be a 1 in 3 chance instead.

 # What Your Score Means

Based on your score, you may, or may not, qualify for credit at your specific institution. The current ACE recommended score for this exam is 400. Your school may require a higher or lower score to receive credit. To find out what score you need for credit, you need to get that information from your school's website or academic advisor.

You lose no points for incorrect questions so make sure you answer each question. If you don't know, make an educated guess. On this particular test, you must answer 100 questions in 90 minutes.

Test Preparation

How much you need to study depends on your knowledge of a subject area. If you are interested in literature, took it in school, or enjoy reading then your study and preparation for the literature or humanities test will not need to be as intensive as that of someone who is new to literature.

This book is much different than the regular CLEP study guides. This book actually teaches you the information that you need to know to pass the test. If you are particularly interested in an area, or feel that you want more information, do a quick search online. We've tried not to include too much depth in areas that are not as essential on the test. It is important to understand all major theories and concepts listed in the table of contents. It is also important to know any bolded words.

Don't worry if you do not understand or know a lot about the area. With minimal study, you can complete and pass the test.

One of the fallacies of other test books is test questions. People assume that the content of the questions are similar to what will be on the test. That is not the case. They are only there to test your "test taking skills" so for those who know to read a question carefully, there is not much added value from taking a "fake" test. So we have constructed our test questions differently. We will use them to teach you new information not covered in the study guide AND to test your knowledge of items you should already know from reading the text. If you don't know the answer to the test question, review the material. If it is new information, then this is an area that will be covered on the test but not in detail.

To prepare for the test, make a series of goals. Allot a certain amount of time to review the information you have already studied and to learn additional material. Take notes as you study; it will help you learn the material. If you haven't done so already, download the study tips guide from the website and use it to start your study plan.

Legal Note

DSST is a registered trademark of The Thomson Corporation and its affiliated companies, and does not endorse this book.

FLASHCARDS

This section contains flashcards for you to use to further your understanding of the material and test yourself on important concepts, names or dates. Read the term or question then flip the page over to check the answer on the back. Keep in mind that this information may not be covered in the text of the study guide. Take your time to study the flashcards, you will need to know and understand these concepts to pass the test.

The Great Society

In what year did Vietnamese lord Ngô Quyên achieve full independence?

What year did the LA Riot break out?

How many years old is Vietnam?

The Buddhist Crisis

Countercultural

The Television War

Ngo Dinh Diem overthrew

938

Johnson's domestic
legislative program

800,000

1964

A term used by historians
to describe any non-
mainstream social culture

A series of protests that
broke out about Diem's
policies

Bai Dai

Another name for the
Vietnam War

Ngo Dinh Diem

Credibility gap

The Strategic Hamlet Program

The New Left

The Fourteen Points

The Domino Theory was coined by

Which university had its students fired upon?

Moratorium to End the War in Vietnam

Contradictions between the news and actual reports generating doubt in the war's success

Became the president of South Vietnam

Intellectual movement

Counterinsurgency program

John Foster Dulles

International political program developed by Woodrow Wilson

Largest anti-war protest during the war

Kent State

Daniel Ellsberg

Who succeeded JFK?

Body count was used as what?

Operation Rolling Thunder

Containment

Ronald Haeberle

Carpet bombing is also known as

Brown v. Board of Education

Lyndon Johnson

Leaked Pentagon reports to the New York Times and The Washington Post

Military air operation

Measure of success

Photo grapher of the My Lai Massacre

Name of the theory in the X article

Separate but equal

Saturation bombing

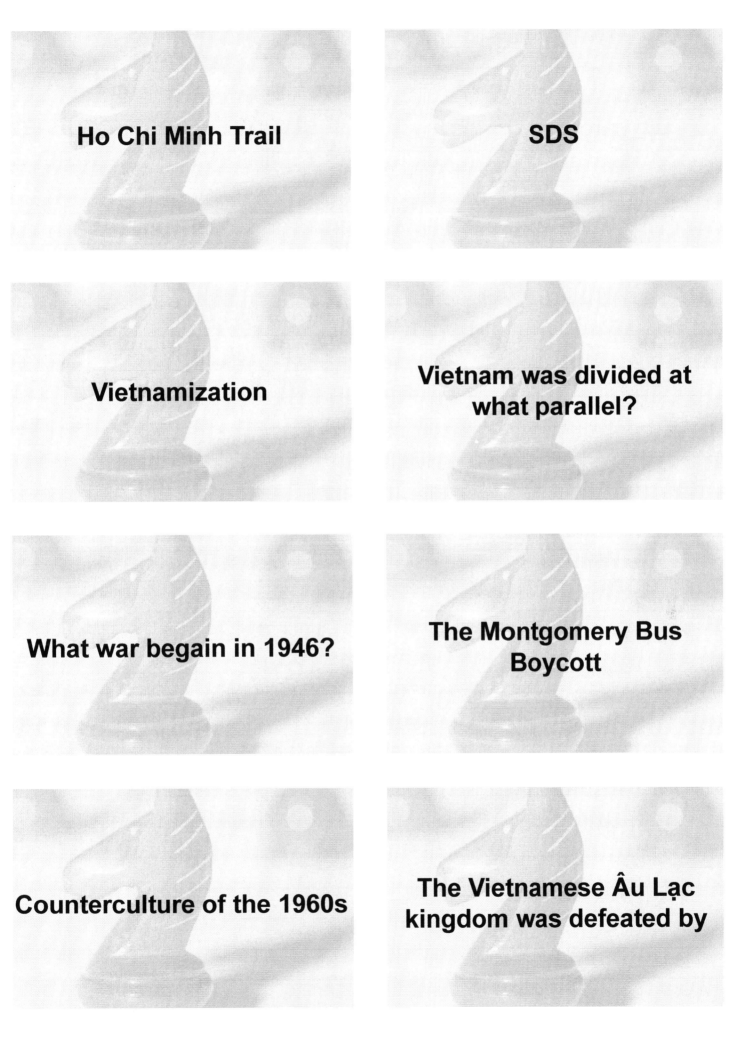

Ho Chi Minh Trail

SDS

Vietnamization

Vietnam was divided at what parallel?

What war begain in 1946?

The Montgomery Bus Boycott

Counterculture of the 1960s

The Vietnamese Âu Lạc kingdom was defeated by

Students for a democratic society

Series of paths, routes and tunnels that the North Vietnamese used to funnel supplies and troops to the Viet Cong

The 17th

Supplying and training of South Vietnamese troops to fight the North on their own with less help from American ground troops

The first major protest of the modern Civil Rights Movement

The First Indochina War

Zhao Tuo

The Hippies

What had begun by around 1000 BCE?

What were the two earliest large-scale political communities in Vietnam?

Nanyue province

Anterior Lỳ dynasty

Before the arrival of Catholicism in the 18th century, what was the dominant religion in Vietnam?

Alexandre de Rhodes

Indochina

Ho Chi Minh

The Văn Lang and
Âu Lạc Kingdoms

Rice cultivation

AD 544 to 602

Composed of modern-
day Northern Vietnam and
the Chinese provinces of
Yunnan, Guangdong, and
Guangxi.

Became the first to attempt
to introduce Christianity
into Vietnam.

Buddhism

Leader of the Vietnamese
Communists and the
Vietcong after WWII

Lands that included
Vietnam, Cambodia, and
Laos

Who was the president and capital of the Democratic State of Vietnam?

When did Mao establish the PRC?

Guerrilla style tactics

Why did the US rush to develop a policy to strengthen the government in South Vietnam?

When did the US start to send economic aid in the form of $216 million to South Vietnam?

When did Ngo Dinh Diem proclaim the creation of the Republic of Vietnam?

Law 10/59

Viet Cong was officially organized when?

1949	Ho Chi Minh and Hanoi
To ensure that communism didn't spread to South Vietnam.	Tactics in which fighters performed multiple hit-and-run attacks, then sunk back into the jungle and villages where they were supported by the people.
October 26, 1955	1955
December 20, 1960	Law created by Diem that made it a capital crime to commit a wide range of political opposition activities.

When were Diem and his brother arrested and executed?

Mekong Delta

What did the Gulf of Tonk Resolution allow President Johnson to do?

Of all American prisoners taken during the war, the highest percentage was from what branch of the military?

When were the first ground troops sent to South Vietnam?

War of attrition

Body count success method

PTSD

The series of provinces at the farthest tip of South Vietnam.

November 2, 1963

Air Force

Order military actions in Southeast Asia without a formal declaration of war.

To win the war, you slowly wear your enemy to the point that their will to fight is no longer there.

22340

Post-traumatic stress disorder

A statistical measure for success that communicated numbers of enemies killed.

Civil Rights Act of 1964

Voting Rights Act of 1965

Loving v. Virginia

When was MLK Jr assassinated?

Draft-dodge

Tet Offensive

Ultimate goal of the Tet Offensive

Silent majority

Prohibited racial discrimination in voting.

Outlawed discrimination based on race, color, religion, sex, or national origin.

1968

Legalized interracial marriage

A surprise attack undertaken by the North Vietnamese across the nation against US and South Vietnamese military centers and cities.

A political statement of opposition in which individuals refused to be conscripted into the growing military forces being sent across the Pacific.

A term Nixon used to refer to those who opposed both the war and the countercultural movement's tactics in opposing the conflict.

To strike a blow at the morale of the US and to convince more people in South Vietnam to support the Communists.

Pentagon Papers	Operation Menu
Paris Peace Accords	Nixon resignation
The Forgotten War	Détente
War Powers Act	Second Indochina War as also known as

A bombing campaign against Communist positions, both along the Vietnamese border and within Cambodia territory.

A classified report which detailed how the American government under Johnson had been continually lying about how well the war was going.

25788

Ended direct American involvement in Vietnam

The relaxing of strained relations in any political situation.

The Korean War

The Vietnam War

A federal law that aimed to remove the president's power to place American troops into combat without getting approval from Congress.